CW00322436

GRAHAM TARRANT

summersdale

THE JOY OF CRICKET

Summersdale Publishers Ltd
46 West Street
Chichester
West Sussex
PO19 1RP
UK

www.summersdale.com

Printed and bound in the Czech Republic

ISBN: 978-1-84953-599-1

Substantial discounts on bulk quantities of Summersdale books are available to corporations, professional associations and other organisations. For details contact Nicky Douglas by telephone: +44 (0) 1243 756902, fax: +44 (0) 1243 786300 or email: nicky@summersdale.com.

For Abigail, Francesca and Rose,
my three cricketing maidens

CONTENTS

INTRODUCTION

The playwright Harold Pinter once referred to cricket as the 'greatest thing that God created on earth' ('certainly greater than sex,' he went on, 'although sex isn't too bad either.'). Indeed for many cricket has a significance that goes beyond the game itself. I can remember the keynote speaker at our school speech day alerting our young minds to the fact that life would bowl us the occasional googly, which we should always endeavour to play with a straight bat. A few years later I heard a clergyman in the Cotswolds inform his congregation that if they wanted to stay in God's good books they shouldn't throw their wicket away with a careless shot. It was their morals he had in mind.

In the days of the British Empire the spirit of cricket was the essence of good sportsmanship, a code of conduct akin to medieval chivalry. Almost any dishonourable behaviour was contemptuously dismissed with the damning phrase: 'It's not cricket'. The notion persisted that the game was a universal force for good. As the Cold War extended its icy grip across the face of the world in the late 1940s, the Catholic Archbishop of Liverpool was heard to observe, 'If Stalin had learned to play cricket the world might now be a better place to live in.'

The truth is that cricket means different things to different people – while remaining totally incomprehensible to countless others, including the French who, despite this, sometimes claim to have invented it. No other sport is as multi-faceted or as rich in history, character and drama. No other sport is as well documented or can match cricket's vast literary output. It is a game of strategic complexity, subtle skills and blatant aggression; though not necessarily at the same time.

The joy of cricket is that there is so much to enjoy – as a player, as a spectator, as a statistician, as a student of the sport's history, or even as an artist like Jocelyn Galsworthy or wicketkeeper-turned-painter Jack Russell. What other sport can be played over five fluctuating days and build to a nail-biting climax such as we've seen in recent times? And the shorter formats of the game have brought their own brand of excitement, especially Twenty20. Some purists resent the introduction of the latter, seeing it as a brash intruder, a corrupting influence. But Twenty20 has brought some much needed money into cricket, has attracted a new and generally younger audience and given the summer game yet another dimension (not least by extending the playing hours).

Of course, not all Test matches and limited-overs games culminate in an exciting climax. Except for the most partisan supporters, outcomes that are too one-sided can dull the appetite, but even then there are likely to be individual performances to admire, promising newcomers to note. And if rain stops play, the wise cricket fan will make sure they have the latest *Wisden* or some other cricketing tome to hand to help soak up the loss of action.

Playing the game is the greatest joy of all. For those, like me, who have never progressed beyond modest club level there are the recurring pleasures of each new season: the fresh ambition to record a personal best; the team camaraderie; the unmistakable sense of carrying on a long tradition. Less sensitive than the professionals

to the weather and state of the pitch, the club cricketer is only too happy to get out there and do their bit. I've been fortunate enough to watch Test cricket around the world, but for my money nothing beats a convivial club game on the village green with afternoon tea lined up in the pavilion and the local pub reassuringly within sight. Cricket at the grass roots.

To do justice to the evolution of cricket, to its milestone events and heroic feats, its memorable characters and off-field dramas, to records set and broken, would take a book many times larger than this. But hopefully this latest addition to the game's ever-expanding library will give a taste of what makes cricket so endlessly fascinating. And such a joy.

CHAPTER 1

CRICKET'S FORMATIVE YEARS

Cricket is the greatest game that the wit of man has yet devised.
SIR PELHAM WARNER (MIDDLESEX AND ENGLAND)

In the beginning

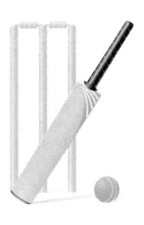

The origins of cricket are lost in the mists of time. No one knows exactly how or where it all began, but by the mid-sixteenth century there is clear evidence of the game being played by children in Surrey as recalled by a witness in a court case in 1598, looking back to his own childhood fifty years before. Also in 1598, an Italian-English dictionary compiled by John Florio refers to playing 'cricket-a-wicket'. The development of the game over the next hundred years was centred in the south-east of England – the counties of Kent, Sussex and Surrey.

Cricket's first known fatality is one Jasper Vinall, whose untimely death took place at Horsted Green, East Sussex, in 1624. He was struck on the head by the batsman, who was trying to hit the ball a second time to avoid being caught.

The English aristocracy and gentry took up the game, attracted as much by its gambling potential as by the sport itself. In the liberated years that followed the restoration of the monarchy in 1660 gambling was rife in all sports, and cricket was no exception. Wealthier patrons sponsored their own teams (often to improve their chances of winning) and employed the best exponents of the game, who became the first professional cricketers. Bats were shaped like the modern hockey stick, the curved base better able to deal with the underarm deliveries that were bowled along the ground. The wicket comprised two stumps with a single bail. Neither the batsman nor the wicketkeeper wore pads or gloves. Scorers kept a tally of the runs by making notches on a stick, every tenth notch cut larger to help with the adding up, and there were four balls to an over.

Prince of cricket

One of cricket's foremost patrons was Frederick Louis, Prince of Wales, son of George II and heir to the throne. An occasional player of questionable skill, he captained Surrey on several occasions and fielded his own team. The Hanover-born prince's love of sport, gambling and women endeared him to the more rakish section of society but not to his own family. There was a notable absence of grieving on their part when Frederick died in 1751 of a burst abscess in the lung, believed to have been caused by a blow from a cricket ball. Thus England was deprived of its first cricketing monarch.

In 1744, the first written laws of cricket were produced, replacing the various verbal rules of engagement that had prevailed until then. The length of the pitch was established as 22 yards (or 1 agricultural chain), unchanged to this day. Other laws drawn up by the London Star and Garter Club, whose headquarters was the Artillery Ground near Finsbury Park, included the height of the stumps, the weight of the ball, the requirement for fielders to appeal for a dismissal, and the stipulation that wicketkeepers must remain stationary and quiet until the ball has been delivered – clearly some sledging had been going on.

As the game evolved, new laws and tactics were introduced. Instead of just rolling the ball along the ground, bowlers now began to give their deliveries some air. The old style of bat was replaced by a straighter version, better suited to combat a flighted or bouncing ball. When

Thomas White of Reigate took guard with a bat wider than the wicket, the lawmakers moved in. In 1771, the width of the bat was restricted to 4¼ inches, still the regulation size today. Three years later the first leg before wicket (lbw) law made it into the rulebook, and soon after a third stump became mandatory.

Thomas Lord, a Yorkshireman and a professional bowler, opened his first cricket ground at Dorset Square in Marylebone (the enterprise was underwritten by two other lords, this time of the realm). Lord fenced off the land and charged the viewing public sixpence to get in. The same year, 1787, saw the formation of the Marylebone Cricket Club (MCC), which gradually took over the administration of the game. When Dorset Square became the haunt of cut-throats, Lord uprooted to St John's Wood; but his second ground was short-lived, the land being commissioned by the authorities for the construction of the Regent's Canal. In 1814, he moved again, just a few hundred yards down the road, to the site of the present Lord's Cricket Ground.

A year after its formation the MCC revised the laws of cricket and began to assert its authority over the game. Beyond the gaze of the club's socially elite membership cricket's rough edges would be visible for some time. But gradually, up and down the country, local enthusiasts formed their own clubs and adopted the new rules. It would be another hundred years before county cricket was properly established, but the game was taking on the shape of an organised sport.

Cricket at Hambledon

Prior to the emergence of the MCC, the most influential cricket club in England was that of the Hampshire village of Hambledon. Run by local landed gentry who recruited the best professional cricketers, the club's ground was on Broadhalfpenny Down, opposite the Bat & Ball Inn whose landlord Richard Nyren captained the side. Other notable players included William ('Silver Billy') Beldham, arguably the greatest batsman of the underarm era; John Small, whose own illustrious batting career spanned forty years; and the all-rounder Tom Taylor. All are immortalised in John (son of Richard) Nyren's The Cricketers of My Time, *the game's first literary classic.*

Bowlers were becoming frustrated by the limitations of the underarm technique. None more so than John Willes of Kent, who was in the habit of getting in some batting practice against the bowling of his sister, Christina. Her voluminous skirt forced her to deliver the ball round-arm which, Willes noticed, made it more difficult to play. When, in 1822, he opened the bowling for Kent against the MCC at Lord's with a similar round-arm action he was promptly no-balled for throwing; the first in the history of the game. Other bowlers followed Willes's initiative however, and six years later the MCC bowed to the inevitable and permitted the bowling arm to be raised level with the elbow.

By this time cricket had fanned out across the land – and across the globe as English settlers and administrators took the game to the far-flung outposts of the British Empire and to the former colony that was now the USA. It was in America that the first official international match was played in 1844. Billed as 'United States of America versus British Empire's Canadian Province', the two-innings game at the St George's Cricket Club in New York was watched by a crowd of 10,000. Canada came out victorious in a low-scoring encounter that generated $120,000 in bets.

Worthy of Wisden

John Wisden, founder of the famous Cricketers'
Almanack, *was one of England's foremost players of
the time. He took over 1,100 wickets in his career,
mostly for Sussex, bowling a mixture of round-arm
pace and slow underarm. In 1850, playing for the
North in a match against the South, he clean bowled
all ten of the opposition with his off-breaks, a feat that
has never been emulated. On the first ever overseas
tour, to Canada and the USA in 1859, he performed
a double hat-trick, taking six wickets in six balls. But
in the final analysis it is his publishing achievement
that will always be best remembered.*

Enter 'The Champion'

It is impossible to overstate the impact Dr William Gilbert Grace had on the game of cricket. An amateur with the mindset of a professional, he quite simply transformed the game. For the last thirty years of the nineteenth century he dominated the sport and in the process made himself one of the most celebrated Englishmen of all time. A native of Gloucestershire, born in the politically turbulent year of 1848, he had an imposing physique and an insatiable appetite for runs and wickets – and for sport in general. The familiar portraits of him with a long, straggly beard and portly girth, bent over a bat that seems several sizes too small, disguise the fact that he was a superb athlete. At the age of 18, having just scored an undefeated 224 for All England against Surrey at The Oval, he left the match halfway through to compete in the national quarter-mile hurdle championship at the Crystal Palace, which he won in record time. To keep fit, he ran cross-country with a pack of beagles and he once threw a cricket ball 117 yards (107 metres). Towards the end of his cricketing days he took up bowls and for five years captained the national team.

'W. G.' didn't rewrite the record books, he created them. His amazing batting achievements were garnered on pitches that were at best unpredictable, at worst downright dangerous. Rib-crunching bouncers were mixed with deliveries that barely rose above ground level. Grace punished the short balls and unerringly blocked the shooters. Few bowlers were spared; many were afraid to bowl within his long, devastating reach. His own bowling was a round-arm medium pace, skilfully flighted and drifting in from leg. He was a brilliant fielder anywhere, but especially off his own bowling.

He captained Gloucestershire CCC for the first twenty-nine years of its existence, three times winning the Championship title outright, the only occasions in the club's history. His Test career spanned twenty years (thirteen times as captain) and started with a century, the first by an England batsman. Two of his brothers also played for their country: Dr E. M. Grace ('The Coroner') and G. F. Grace, who tragically died shortly after making his Test debut. W. G.'s commanding presence at the crease daunted bowlers and umpires alike. On one famous occasion during a minor match, having been bowled first ball, Grace calmly replaced the bail and informed the dumbstruck bowler, 'They've come to see me bat, not you bowl'. And he was right, of course. He played his last first-class game in 1908, by which time he had amassed over 54,000 runs and taken 2,800 wickets. Not bad for a man who for much of the time was a busy medical practitioner.

First-class records set by Dr W. G. Grace

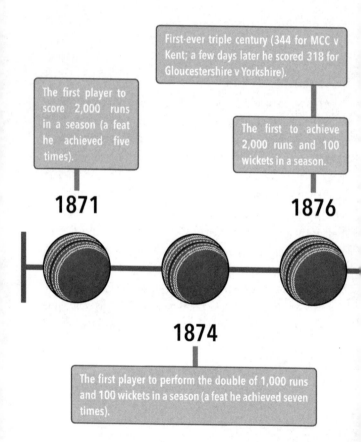

First-ever triple century (344 for MCC v Kent; a few days later he scored 318 for Gloucestershire v Yorkshire).

The first player to score 2,000 runs in a season (a feat he achieved five times).

The first to achieve 2,000 runs and 100 wickets in a season.

1871

1876

1874

The first player to perform the double of 1,000 runs and 100 wickets in a season (a feat he achieved seven times).

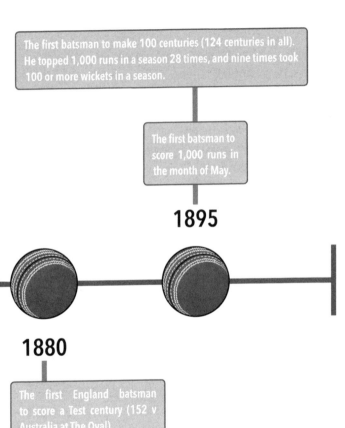

The first batsman to make 100 centuries (124 centuries in all). He topped 1,000 runs in a season 28 times, and nine times took 100 or more wickets in a season.

The first batsman to score 1,000 runs in the month of May.

1895

1880

The first England batsman to score a Test century (152 v Australia at The Oval).

The Golden Age

The first Test between England and Australia (not yet playing for the Ashes) took place in Melbourne in 1877. Facing the very first ball in Test cricket was Australia's opening batsman Charles Bannerman, who had been born twenty-five years earlier in what is now the London suburb of Woolwich. He went on to score 165 ('retired hurt') and Australia won the inaugural match by 45 runs. England levelled the two-match series a couple of weeks later and sailed back to England with honours even. It was the start of a rivalry that has never lost its intensity or competitive bite.

   Cricket, though restricted to the summer months, was now the most popular sport in England, drawing crowds that modern organisers can only dream about. Amateurs and professionals, who had totally separate lives and living standards off the field, played alongside each other (and in opposition in the annual Gentlemen v Players fixture). County cricket was booming (the County Championship was formally constituted in 1890 as a competition between eight first-class counties; by the end of the decade there were seven more) and producing a new generation of star cricketers. The W. G. Grace era was coming to an end, in 'The Doctor's' last Test in 1899 (he was now nearly 51 years old), two future all-time greats made their international debuts: Wilfred Rhodes of Yorkshire and Australia's Victor Trumper.

As the world moved to a new century, cricket entered its so-called Golden Age. In truth, it was probably no more 'golden' than any other age, but when viewed from the aftermath of World War One it took on a nostalgic glow of endlessly long summers playing host to cricket matches contested in the finest spirit of the game. There was a characteristic north-south divide amongst the players. Yorkshire boasted its gritty professional all-rounders, Wilfred Rhodes and George Hirst (though the county was captained by the autocratic Lord Hawke). Genteel Sussex-by-the-sea had the elegant Kumar Shri Ranjitsinhji, His Highness the Jam Sahib of Nawanagar (or 'Ranji' for short), and C. B. Fry, an all-round amateur sportsman par excellence – world record holder at the long jump, an England cap at soccer and, but for an untimely injury, an Oxford Blue at rugby. Together they piled on the runs for Sussex and England. Ranji was the first Indian to play Test cricket; Fry in later life would be offered the throne of Albania. You couldn't make it up.

Somewhere in between came Gloucestershire's Gilbert Jessop, nicknamed 'The Croucher' because of his hunched stance at the crease. Jessop was a phenomenal striker of the ball, six times getting to a first-class century in under an hour, the fastest of them in 40 minutes. In 1902, he steered England to a legendary victory against Australia, clouting a second-innings hundred in 75 minutes, just when all had appeared lost. When he was finally dismissed with 15 runs still needed to win, Wilfred Rhodes, the last man in, joined his fellow Yorkshireman George Hirst at the wicket. It is then that Hirst is said to have uttered the immortal words: 'We'll get them in singles, Wilfred.' They did, and England were victors by one wicket.

Australia had its own stars: Clem Hill, the first player to be dismissed for 99 in a Test match (though he more than made up for it later) and the incomparable Victor Trumper, a spectacular stroke-maker and the first to score a Test hundred before lunch. When Trumper died in 1915 at the age of 37, 20,000 people lined the streets of Sydney to pay their last respects and 11 former teammates carried his coffin into the church. Archie MacLaren, one of England's premier batsmen of the time, said: 'Compared to Victor, I was a cab-horse to a Derby winner.'

Cricket had come a long way from its tentative beginnings with bat and ball. The next hundred years would see many changes to the sport, and the coming and going of many great players. But it was now recognisably the game we play today.

Cricket in the saddle

The following advertisement appeared in the *Kentish Gazette* on 29 April 1794:

Cricketing on Horseback.

A very singular game of cricket will be played on Tuesday the 6th of May in Linstead Park between the Gentlemen of the Hill and the Gentlemen of the Dale, for one guinea a man. The whole to be performed on horseback. To begin at 9 o'clock, and the game to be played out. A good ordinary [meal] on the ground by John Hogben.

Some notable dates in cricket history

First Gentlemen v Players match.

Cricket is mentioned in John Florio's Italian-English dictionary, *A Worlde of Wordes*.

Thomas Lord opens what is now the current Lord's Cricket Ground.

First recorded case of a dismissal 'leg before wicket' (Surrey v 13 of England).

Formation of Marylebone Cricket Club.

18
1806
1795
1787
1744
1709
1598

First written laws of the game.

First recorded county match: Kent v Surrey.

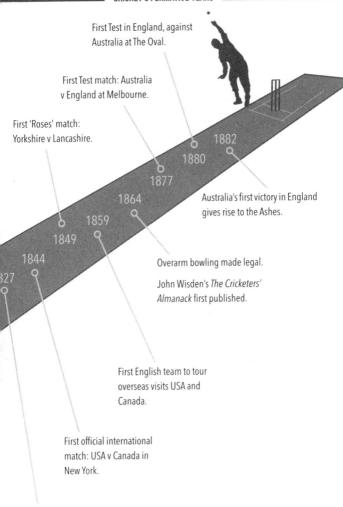

First Test in England, against
Australia at The Oval.

First Test match: Australia
v England at Melbourne.

First 'Roses' match:
Yorkshire v Lancashire.

1882

1880

1877

1864

1859

1849

1844

327

Australia's first victory in England
gives rise to the Ashes.

Overarm bowling made legal.

John Wisden's *The Cricketers'
Almanack* first published.

First English team to tour
overseas visits USA and
Canada.

First official international
match: USA v Canada in
New York.

First Oxford v Cambridge
match.

Some notable dates in cricket history

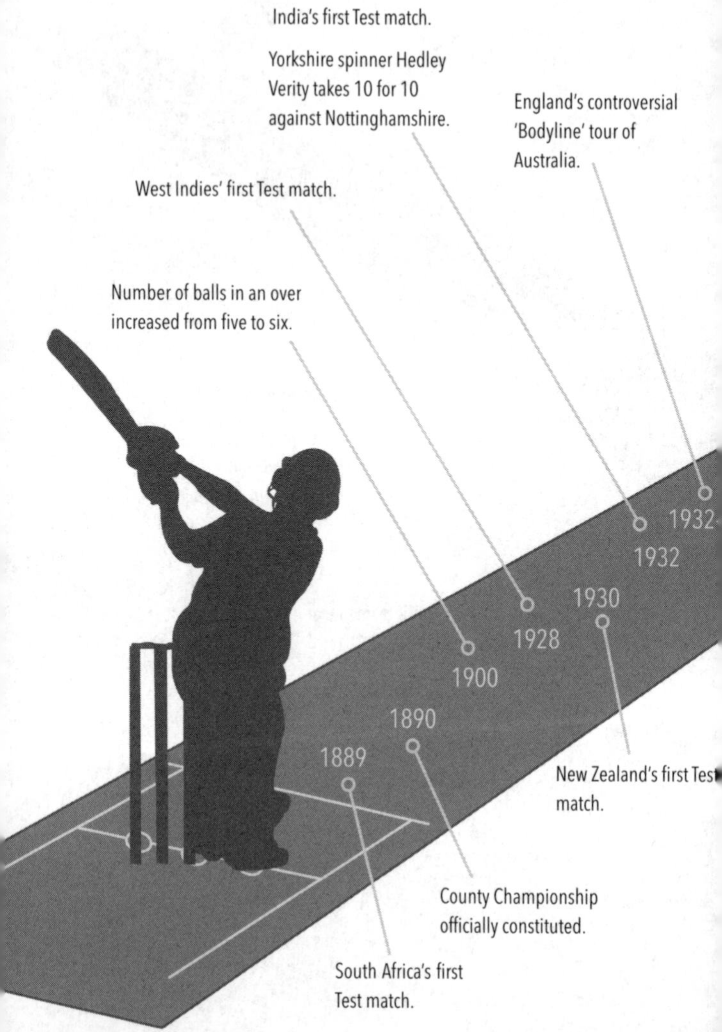

India's first Test match.

Yorkshire spinner Hedley Verity takes 10 for 10 against Nottinghamshire.

England's controversial 'Bodyline' tour of Australia.

West Indies' first Test match.

Number of balls in an over increased from five to six.

1932

1932

1930

1928

1900

1890

1889

New Zealand's first Test match.

County Championship officially constituted.

South Africa's first Test match.

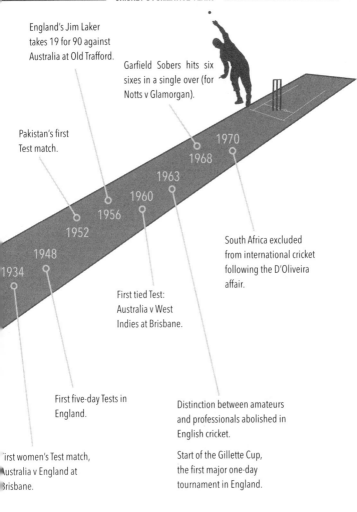

England's Jim Laker takes 19 for 90 against Australia at Old Trafford.

Garfield Sobers hits six sixes in a single over (for Notts v Glamorgan).

Pakistan's first Test match.

1970
1968
1963
1960
1956
1952
1948
1934

South Africa excluded from international cricket following the D'Oliveira affair.

First tied Test: Australia v West Indies at Brisbane.

First five-day Tests in England.

Distinction between amateurs and professionals abolished in English cricket.

Start of the Gillette Cup, the first major one-day tournament in England.

First women's Test match, Australia v England at Brisbane.

Some notable dates in cricket history

Australian Graham Yallop is the first to
wear a protective helmet in a Test match.

Sri Lanka's first Test match.

Centenary Test at Melbourne produces
identical result to original match.

Australian media tycoon Kerry Packer
launches his World Series Cricket.

The eight-ball over is
abolished in Australia.

1980

1978

1977

1975

1973

1971

England hosts the
inaugural Prudential
World Cup.

First women's World Cup
is staged in England.

First one-day
international: Australia v
England at Melbourne.

Pakistan forfeits the Oval Test after being accused of ball tampering.

Andrew Strauss becomes Shane Warne's 700th Test wicket.

Twenty20 Cup launched in England.

2013

2007

2006

2004

2003

2000

1998

1994

2

Sachin Tendulkar retires from cricket after his 200th Test match.

First ICC World Twenty20 takes place in South Africa.

Brian Lara is the first to score 400 in a Test innings (v England in Antigua).

MCC votes to admit women as members after 211 years.

South Africa's captain Hansie Cronje is banned from cricket for life after match-fixing.

Bangladesh's first Test match.

County Championship split into two divisions, with promotion and relegation.

Brian Lara scores 501 not out for Warwickshire v Durham.

Zimbabwe's first Test match.

Durham attains first-class status, the first county since Glamorgan in 1921.

Play the game

For those new to cricket or wishing to play something other than the traditional game, the ECB (England and Wales Cricket Board) has some stimulating suggestions. These include weatherproof indoor cricket; Last Man Stands, an eight-a-side version of Twenty20; and Easy Cricket, a casual approach to the game that's ideal for all the family.
www.ecb.co.uk

Fielding positions

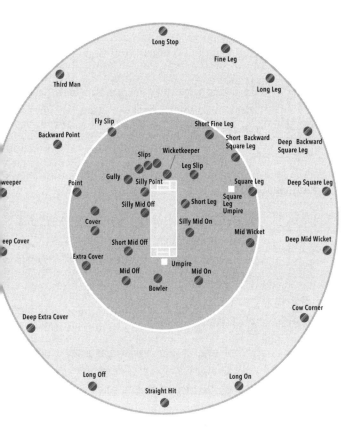

Different types of cricket

Test cricket

The longest form of the game, played between national sides with matches taking place over five days. There are currently ten Test-playing countries.

First-class cricket

Matches of three or four days' duration – e.g. the County Cricket Championship in England and Wales. There are equivalent first-class competitions in all the major cricketing nations.

Limited-overs cricket

Single-innings matches usually completed in one day and with a fixed number of overs per side – typically 40, 50 or 60. Between countries the fixtures are known as one-day internationals or ODIs.

Twenty20 cricket

Introduced in 2003, this is an even shorter version of the game with 20 overs allocated per innings. There are domestic and international competitions similar to those for the longer limited-overs format.

Amateur cricket

The grass roots of the sport, usually confined to weekend activity. Standards vary hugely, from club cricket of near professional class to less structured encounters where enjoyment ranks higher than skill.

The ten Test-playing countries

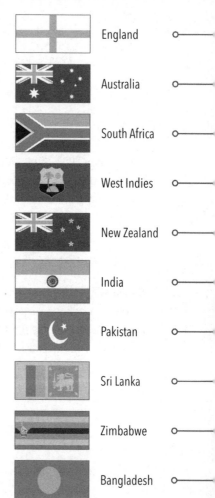

England   o——

Australia   o——

South Africa   o——

West Indies   o——

New Zealand   o——

India   o——

Pakistan   o——

Sri Lanka   o——

Zimbabwe   o——

Bangladesh   o——

Inaugural Test

v Australia at Melbourne, March 1877

v England at Melbourne, March 1877

v England at Port Elizabeth, March 1889

v England at Lord's, June 1928

v England at Christchurch, January 1930

v England at Lord's, June 1932

v India at Delhi, October 1952

v England at Colombo, February 1982

v India at Harare, October 1992

v India at Dhaka, November 2000

BIRTH OF
THE ASHES

You've got normal Test cricket, and then you've got Ashes cricket.
IAN BELL (WARWICKSHIRE AND ENGLAND)

For English and Australian cricket followers nothing matters more than the Ashes. The coveted trophy for which the two countries compete represents the game at its highest level and remains its greatest prize. The challenge, passed on from generation to generation, has produced individual performances that have become the stuff of legend – Laker at Old Trafford, Massie at Lord's, Botham at Headingley, Pietersen at The Oval, Bradman just about everywhere – and some of cricket's most dramatic climaxes. None more so than the match that started it all.

Cricketing mercenary

The only cricketer to have represented both Australia and England against each other is W. E. ('Billy') Midwinter, a Gloucestershire-born all-rounder who played for his adopted country, Australia, in the first-ever Test in 1877. He toured England two years later and was forcibly persuaded by W. G. Grace, who intercepted him at Lord's just as he was about to take the field, to leave the touring party there and then and to come and play for his native county. Midwinter stayed with Gloucestershire for several seasons, returning to Australia as an England player in 1881–82. In all he played eight times for Australia and four times for England, and anticipated the modern cricketing mercenary by commuting between Gloucestershire and Victoria over a number of years.

England demonised

The 1882 Oval Test match was the only one that summer and only the second played in England. There was enormous interest in the match, 20,000 people – the largest crowd ever to attend a game of cricket – turning up on the first day. England had selected their strongest side, with the massively reassuring figure of W. G. Grace at the top of the order. All the Australians had previous Test experience but with home advantage England were favourites to win.

On a rain-affected pitch, Australia were shot out for 63, their lowest score of the tour; but England failed to take advantage of the situation, mustering only 101 in reply. The Australian fast bowler F. R. Spofforth, whose mesmerising performances with the ball (including the first-ever Test hat-trick) had won him the nickname 'The Demon', did most of the damage. An ability to generate late movement in the air and off the pitch, coupled with a deceptive change of pace, confounded the English batsmen. His 7 for 46 included the prize wicket of W. G. Grace, clean bowled for four. The pendulum swung back England's way when the opposition was dismissed in their second innings for a paltry 122. Perhaps still sore about his own cheap dismissal, W. G. resorted to an unattractive piece of gamesmanship in running out Sammy Jones, when the Australian batsman momentarily strayed from his crease to pat down the pitch. It all added to the tension, but with just 85 runs needed to win, the odds were firmly with the home side.

Before taking the field for the final innings the irrepressible Fred Spofforth urged on his teammates: 'This thing can be done.' However, at 57 for 2, and with Grace still batting, England seemed to be coasting home. Then they hit the rocks. The man who said it could be done, did it. Spofforth (bowling the mandatory four-ball overs) ripped through the England side, taking four wickets for two runs in his last 11 overs and seven wickets in all. Australia were the winners by seven runs and 'The Demon' had match figures of 14 for 90. Cheering spectators, by no means all of them Australian, carried him shoulder high up the pavilion steps. One man stayed in his seat, dead of heart failure. One of the most exciting matches in cricket history was all over in two days.

Four days later *The Sporting Times* published its famous mock obituary and unwittingly gave a name to cricket's most cherished trophy:

In Affectionate Remembrance
of
ENGLISH CRICKET,
which died at the Oval
on
29th AUGUST, 1882,

Deeply lamented by a large
circle of sorrowing
friends and acquaintances.

R.I.P.

N.B. – The body will be
cremated and the ashes
taken to Australia.

Demon from down under

Fred Spofforth's strikingly stern features, with a heavy black moustache and piercing dark eyes, enhanced his image as a demon fast bowler, though off the field he was an engaging character and lively raconteur. Well over six feet tall and athletically built he could run a hundred yards in under 11 seconds. On one occasion he made a 400-mile round trip on horseback to play in an up-country cricket match in Australia, taking all 20 opposition wickets and all of them clean bowled.

The urn

At the end of 1882, the Honourable Ivo Bligh (later Lord Darnley)
captained the England team to Australia, with three Test matches
initially scheduled. Australia won the first, at Melbourne – the match
originally billed as 'Mr Murdoch's Eleven v The Hon. Ivo F. W. Bligh's
Team' – but England fought back to take the next two. A fourth
match was then arranged for which, bizarrely, the captains agreed to
experiment by using a separate pitch for each of the four innings.
Australia won.

Before leaving England the aristocratic Bligh had vowed to bring
back the mythical 'ashes of English cricket'. At some point after
the conclusion of the third Test (the actual details vary according
to different accounts), a group of Melbourne ladies whimsically
presented him with a 6-inch (15-cm) terracotta urn containing ashes.
A red velvet bag in which to keep it came later. Attached to the urn
were a few lines of doggerel clipped from a Melbourne publication,
cheerfully commemorating some of the England team.

No one knows for sure what the ashes had originally been. One theory was a stump, another the outer casing of a ball. Many years later, Lord Darnley's by now elderly daughter stated that it was her mother-in-law's wedding veil that had been sacrificed. But the general consensus is that the powdery remains are most likely those of a single bail.

Despite all this, it was another twenty years before 'the Ashes' became an established part of cricket's vocabulary, *Wisden* first giving them a mention in 1905. After Ivo Bligh's death in 1927, his widow gave the precious urn to the MCC and it can now be seen in the museum at Lord's. Too fragile to be manhandled by victorious captains the urn has never been used as a trophy, though a number of replicas have been held aloft for public acclamation. Since 1998, a Waterford Crystal representation of the urn has served as the official Ashes Trophy.

End of an innings

The former Lancashire all-rounder R. G. 'Dick' Barlow played 17 times for England and took part in the 1882 Test match that gave rise to the Ashes. He is named in the commemorative verse on the side of the Ashes urn and, along with Lancashire and England opening partner A. N. Hornby, is immortalised in Francis Thompson's celebrated poem 'At Lord's' ('O my Hornby and my Barlow long ago!'). Barlow died in 1919 at the age of 68. The inscription on his tombstone reads: 'Bowled At Last'.

Worthy opponents

After 132 years and 320 matches fought out on opposite sides of the world, the spoils are almost equally divided: 32 series wins to Australia, 31 to England and 5 drawn. Australia however has a significant lead in terms of match results: 128 to 103 with 89 Tests drawn.

Both countries have had periods of domination. For the first 15 years of Ashes cricket it was practically all England. Then honours were fairly even until the Bradman era, the Bodyline series of 1932–33 being England's only success in almost twenty years. England finally wrested back the Ashes in the Coronation year of 1953, but by the end of the decade they were once again in Australia's possession. The sixties belonged to Australia; most of the seventies and eighties to England.

Ashes extra

Australia were victorious in every Ashes series between 1990 and 2003, winning a total of 24 Tests to England's seven (six were drawn).

England's 2–1 victory in 2005 was their first series win against Australia for 18 years.

Australia's 5–0 defeat of England in 2006–07 was only the second such whitewash in Ashes history. The first was in 1920–21, when England were again on the receiving end.

England won three consecutive Ashes series between 2009 and 2013, the first time they had achieved the feat since 1981.

England's 5–0 thrashing in 2013–14 was statistically the worst of their three whitewashes, losing three of the Tests by a margin of over 200 runs.

Wicketkeeper-batsmen

The first wicketkeeper to score a century in an Ashes Test was England's Leslie Ames, who made 120 at Lord's in 1934. It was to be 40 years before another man of Kent, Alan Knott, equalled his feat. The first Australian wicketkeeper to make an Ashes ton was Rodney Marsh, in the 1977 Centenary Test. In 2006, Aussie thumper-stumper Adam Gilchrist scored the second fastest Test hundred ever, his century coming in 57 balls. In 2013-14, Brad Haddin set a new record for the most runs by a wicketkeeper in an Ashes series, his aggregate of 493 (61.62) easily overhauling Alec Stewart's previous total of 378.

THE DON

*Every ball is for me the first ball, whether
my score is zero or two hundred.*

SIR DONALD BRADMAN

No survey of the history of cricket, however brief, can leave out the Australian Sir Donald Bradman, whose first-class career lasted from 1927 to 1949. Cricketers, like anyone else, can only properly be judged in the context of their time, tempting though it is to make comparisons across different eras. Bradman is often referred to as the greatest batsman of them all, but the only thing that can be stated with absolute certainty is that he was the best of his time. That said, his statistics are unlikely ever to be equalled. In a first-class career spanning twenty years he averaged 95.14 per innings; in Test matches 99.94.

Sadly, we are left with only black and white newsreel footage of the man in action. But what there is clearly demonstrates the Don's nimble footwork, his array of shots around the wicket (many of them unorthodox), his immaculate timing and perfect placement. Of modest height (5 ft 7 in) and build, he hit the ball with tremendous power. The runs flowed from his bat in all directions, with a speed and certainty that drove bowlers to distraction. He wasn't infallible, but he was the next best thing.

On his first tour of England in 1930, he scored a hundred in the first Test at Trent Bridge, a double century at Lord's in the next, followed by a triple century in the third Test at Headingley. In the latter match, 309 of his runs came on the first day (still a record), including a hundred before lunch. He was a month short of his twenty-second birthday. Desperate to combat Bradman on the next tour Down Under, England devised the infamous bodyline theory, in which fast bowlers would target the batsman's body rather than the wicket. It succeeded to the extent that Bradman was restricted to an average of 56.57, meagre by his standards, with England winning the series 4–1. But the triumph was short-lived. The outcry surrounding England's brutal tactics resulted in a change in the laws of cricket and by the time the two sides met again, in 1934, normal services had been resumed, with Bradman registering another double and triple hundred in the series.

Don Bradman was 40 years of age when he made his fourth and final tour of England as captain of the so-called 'Invincibles'. Like many of his contemporaries he had lost six playing years to the war (and in his case to ill health) and was said to be past his best. Perhaps he was, but he still managed to score two Test hundreds, one of which helped steer Australia to an improbable victory at Headingley. Set to score 404 in 344 minutes to win on a pitch taking spin (Jim Laker was part of England's attack), they knocked off the runs with half an hour to spare, Bradman's contribution 173 not out.

His final Test outing came at The Oval in a match that Australia already had in the bag, having dismissed England for 52 in their first innings. The crowd applauded him all the way to the wicket, where the England captain Norman Yardley led his team in three cheers for the Don. The second ball he received from Eric Hollies was a googly and clean bowled him. Commentating at the time, John Arlott said: 'I wonder if you see a ball very clearly… when the opposing team has just stood round you and given you three cheers and the crowd has clapped you all the way to the wicket. I wonder if you see the ball at all.' Bradman was four runs short of a career Test average of 100, a statistical nicety that he was unaware of at the time. Possibly just as well.

With so much of the focus inevitably on his batting, it is easy to forget that Bradman was a brilliant outfielder (for his time) and an astute captain. Ironically, given the punishment he routinely dished out to their bowlers, the British public loved him. When he arrived in England in 1948 there were 500 fan letters awaiting him. He personally answered every one. For Australians during the economically depressed years of the thirties he was an inspiration, drawing huge crowds wherever he went. A great ambassador for the game as well as a great player, he seldom let them down.

Some statistical highlights:

In 1938–39, he scored six hundreds in consecutive first-class matches.

Of his 117 centuries in first-class cricket, 31 were double hundreds, five were triple and there was one quadruple.

On average, one in every three Bradman innings produced a century.

He twice scored a thousand runs in England before the end of May.

On each of his four tours of England he played in the traditional opening fixture against Worcestershire, recording scores of 236, 206, 258 and 107.

Following his second-ball duck in his final Test innings, Bradman finished the England tour with consecutive scores of 150, 143 and 153.

His 452 not out for NSW against Queensland remains unbeaten in Australia.

In 1948 he became the first Australian cricketer to be knighted.

At The Oval in 1934 Bradman and Bill Ponsford put on 451 for the second wicket, breaking their own record of 388 set in the previous Test. Bradman's contributions were 304 and 244 respectively.

In the 52 Tests in which he played, Bradman scored over 25 per cent of the team's total runs, and averaged more than three times the combined average of the other batsmen.

The Don v some modern greats

		Tests	Innings	Runs	Average
Don Bradman	(AU)	52	80	6,996	99.94
Jacques Kallis	(SA)	166	280	13,289	55.37
Sachin Tendulkar	(IND)	200	329	15,921	53.78
Brian Lara	(WI)	131	232	11,953	52.88
Ricky Ponting	(AU)	168	287	13,378	51.85
Sunil Gavaskar	(IND)	125	214	10,122	51.12
Allan Border	(AU)	156	265	11,174	50.56
Vivian Richards	(WI)	121	182	8,540	50.23
Kevin Pietersen	(ENG)	104	181	8,181	47.28

CHAPTER 4

MASTERCLASS

*He can play in any era and at any level. I
would say he's 99.5 per cent perfect.*

VIV RICHARDS ON SACHIN TENDULKAR

Every era has produced its master cricketers, players who have stood
at the pinnacle of the sport: W. G. Grace, Victor Trumper, Jack Hobbs,

Wilfred Rhodes and Staffordshire
bowling legend Sydney Barnes – who
in the years before the First World War
took 189 wickets for England in 27
Tests, leading some to believe that
he was the greatest bowler of them
all.

While Australia boasted Don
Bradman, England had its own batting
giants in Wally Hammond and Len Hutton.
Hammond, a professional who switched to amateur status in order
to captain his country, hit 22 centuries in his 85 Tests, the highest of
them 336 not out, made against New Zealand in 1933. Hutton, later
England's first professional captain, hoisted a record 364 against
Australia at The Oval in 1938, a score that remained unbeaten for

twenty years. In the Caribbean, the spectacular George Headley was known as the 'Black Bradman', more for his prolific scoring than his batting style.

In the post-war years, other Test-playing countries began to make their mark, though Australia and England still dominated the scene. For Australia, Ray Lindwall and Keith Miller were a masterly pair of pace bowlers, while England's attack rested on the broad shoulders of the indefatigable Alec Bedser. As decade followed decade other great English players emerged, Peter May and Colin Cowdrey, Fred Trueman and Brian Statham, and the off-spinner Jim Laker whose 19 for 90 at Old Trafford in 1956 will surely never be surpassed. Australia produced Arthur Morris and Neil Harvey and later the Chappell brothers, Ian and Greg, both successful captains of their country. From South Africa, where world-class slow bowlers have generally been in short supply, came off-spinner Hugh Tayfield; and the West Indies donated the extraordinary batting trio, the 'Three Ws' – (Everton) Weekes, (Frank) Worrell and (Clyde) Walcott – and probably the greatest all-rounder in the history of the game, Garfield Sobers.

It was Sobers who finally overtook Len Hutton's record Test score, amassing 365 not out against Pakistan in 1958 (he followed it up with innings of 125 and 109 not out in the next Test). Later, he became the first batsman to hit six sixes in a single first-class over. As a left-arm bowler he possessed three equally effective styles: fast medium, orthodox spin and unorthodox spin in the form of googlies and 'chinamen'. And there has been no better close to the wicket fieldsman.

Many more great players arrived on the scene in the sixties and seventies – too many to include in a survey of this length. The South African Graeme Pollock (brother of fast bowler Peter and uncle to all-rounder Shaun) was the finest left-handed batsman of his time. Pakistan and India each produced a pocket-sized master opener, Hanif Mohammad and Sunil Gavaskar; while England had the inimitable Geoffrey Boycott, for so long his country's first and often last line of defence.

From the mid-seventies to the early nineties, their peak years, West Indies had a superabundance of talent in all departments of the game. A production line of lethal fast bowlers from Andy Roberts to Courtney Walsh unmercifully battered the opposition. Then it was their batsmen's turn, with the explosive Viv Richards and the bespectacled powerhouse Clive Lloyd more often than not leading the charge.

It was also a fertile period for spin bowlers. Derek Underwood, a deadly left-arm spinner of brisk pace (especially on rain-affected pitches), was regularly England's trump card. Slower, but no less full of guile, was the turbaned Bishan Bedi, the best of an outstanding Indian spin quartet.

The new breed of wicketkeeper-batsman yielded the likes of Alan Knott, Jack Russell and Alec Stewart for England, Ian Healy and later, Adam Gilchrist (the finest practitioner of them all) for Australia, and Mark Boucher for South Africa.

And if all that wasn't enough, the careers of five great all-rounders coincided: Mike Procter (South Africa), Imran Khan (Pakistan), Kapil Dev (India), Richard Hadlee (New Zealand) and Ian Botham (England) – the first male cricketer to score a century and take ten wickets in the same Test match (Australia's Betty Wilson had managed it 22 years earlier, in 1958), an all-round feat that even Garry Sobers failed to achieve.

Twin class

Australia's Waugh twins, Steve and Mark, were a cricketing phenomenon. In Test matches they scored 18,956 runs between them, including 52 centuries. In ODIs the combined total was 16,069 runs with 21 centuries. In addition, Steve captained Australia in 57 Tests (41 of them to victory) and 106 ODIs, winning the 1999 World Cup in the process. How relieved the rest of the cricketing world must have been that Mrs Waugh didn't give birth to triplets.

The twenty-first century is still in its infancy and will doubtless produce many great cricketers of its own. Here are some recent masters of their craft:

Brian Lara

In 1994, within the space of two months, Trinidad's most famous son broke two world records: the highest score in a Test match (375 against England in Antigua) and the highest in any first-class game (501 not out for Warwickshire against Durham at Edgbaston). He notched 34 Test centuries in all, and a further 19 in one-day internationals. As the West Indies side as a whole declined, Lara increasingly played a lone hand. In the 2001–02 series against Sri Lanka, he scored 42 per cent of the team's runs, with a personal tally of 688. Australia's Matthew Hayden eclipsed Lara's record Test score, but not for long. Within six months Lara had reclaimed the top spot, with an innings of 400 not out against hapless England.

At his best, and he frequently was, Lara was a batsman of breathtaking brilliance. But the pressures that came with success, and the strain of propping up a weak West Indian side (much of the time as captain), took their toll. Acrimonious disputes with the administrators added to his problems and accelerated his departure from the game.

Shane Warne

In his first Test for Australia, against India at Sydney in 1992, Shane Warne's bowling stats were 1 for 150 (Sachin Tendulkar had figures of 1 for 2 in the same match, but he bowled 44 overs less). But shrewd judges, among them former Australian captain Richie Benaud, himself an eminent leg-spinner, had spotted something very special about the chubby, blonde Victorian. The legendary delivery that bowled Mike Gatting a year later made their point.

Warne's craftily concealed spinning options bamboozled the best batsmen around, sometimes embarrassingly. He made leg-spin fashionable. Warne was forced to change his bowling action after a shoulder operation in 1998, and swallowing forbidden substances (allegedly in the form of a diuretic to help reduce weight) cost him a year's ban in 2003. But the irrepressible Warne bounced back and carried on where he had left off. He became the first bowler to take 600 Test wickets, then 700. He recorded one Test hat-trick but might have had several more. He rarely had an off day, and if he did the opposition would pay for it later. Behind the razzamatazz was a wily cricket brain and there was no fiercer competitor.

Out spun

Scott Borthwick's debut wicket in the fifth Test at Sydney in 2014 was the first by an England leg-spinner since Ian Salisbury dismissed Inzamam-ul-Haq in the Faisalabad Test in 2000. In roughly the same number of years Australian leggie Shane Warne took 708 Test wickets.

Glenn McGrath

Glenn McGrath was selected for his country after playing in only eight first-class matches. It was the beginning of a Test career that would span thirteen years, during which he became the first fast bowler to be capped 100 times by Australia. His haul of 563 Test wickets comfortably passes the previous record set by a 'quickie' (Courtney Walsh, 519) and places him fourth in the rankings behind his three great spinning contemporaries – Muttiah Muralitharan, Shane Warne and Anil Kumble.

Only Dennis Lillee can challenge him as the greatest Australian fast bowler of the modern era, and possibly of all time. McGrath's metronomic line and length on or about the off stump, and the ability to extract extra bounce from all but the flattest pitches, troubled every batsman who faced him. He was equally effective in one-day internationals and is the leading wicket-taker in the history of the Cricket World Cup. He retired from the game at the end of the 2007 competition, but not before he was adjudged 'Man of the Tournament'.

Sachin Tendulkar

As a 14-year-old schoolboy, Sachin Tendulkar shared a record unbroken partnership of 664 with his friend Vinod Kambli, who would follow him into the Indian team. At fifteen-and-a-half he became the youngest cricketer to score a century on his first-class debut. He made his first Test hundred at the age of 17 and had another 15 under his belt before he was 25. The runs never stopped flowing: 51 Test centuries in all, another 49 in ODIs – including the first-ever double hundred in the shorter format. Bowing out in his 200th Test was yet another statistical milestone.

Tendulkar has been to the modern game what Bradman was in a previous era: put briefly, a nightmare for bowlers. Near technically perfect, adept on any surface and with every shot in the book, he had a hunger for runs that sapped the strength of bowling attacks around the world. The Indian crowds worshipped him. A lesser man would perhaps have wilted under the steamy adoration, but like a prize hothouse bloom, Tendulkar seemed to thrive on it.

Muttiah Muralitharan

Muralitharan's bowling action has been a mixed blessing. Shaped by a deformed elbow, his unusual style of delivery helped to confound batsman while at the same time attracting accusations of throwing. With his rapid wrist movement he extracted more turn than most off-spinners, but it was not until he developed his doosra – a ball that turned the other way or held its line – that he really came into his own. In the 1995 Boxing Day Test, Australian umpire Darrell Hair no-balled him for throwing seven times in three overs. Three years later fellow umpire Ross Emerson repeated the call. Murali's bowling action was scrutinised on film by the authorities and pronounced legitimate, though the debate continued throughout his career.

He overtook Shane Warne's 708 wickets, finishing with a symmetrically satisfying 800 garnered in twelve Tests fewer than his rival (though he did bowl over 3,000 balls more). There were a further 534 wickets in ODIs. Despite often being the only Tamil in the Sri Lankan side during years of bloody ethnic conflict, Murali remained his country's most popular and revered cricketer.

Jacques Kallis

Jacques Kallis may lack the charisma of Shane Warne or the god-like status of Sachin Tendulkar, but he's not short of much else. The most outstanding all-rounder in the modern game, he compiled over 13,000 runs in Tests before retiring from first-class cricket in 2013, and has made close to 12,000 in ODIs. His Test batting average of 55.37 is up there with the very best and his tally of 45 Test hundreds (the last of them coming on cue in his final match) is second only to Tendulkar's. In 2010, at the age of 35 and when most cricketers' glory days are behind them, he scored his maiden Test double hundred and two years later followed it up with another.

His fast-medium bowling has predictably slowed down since he first appeared on the scene, though he can still surprise batsmen with a sudden quicker ball or some extra bounce. His 565 wickets for South Africa are almost equally divided between Test matches and ODIs. And if all that wasn't enough, he pocketed 200 Test catches – the second highest on record.

Master blasters

As the game has quickened in tempo, more master blasters have appeared on the scene: Kevin Pietersen (England), David Warner (Australia), Chris Gayle (West Indies), Brendon McCullum (New Zealand) and M. S. Dhoni (India) among the international stars. Spectacular bouts of hitting have become the norm, especially in the Twenty20 format. New Zealand all-rounder Corey Anderson saw in the 2014 New Year with the fastest-ever century in international cricket, in an ODI against West Indies. His hundred came up in 36 balls (14 sixes and six fours), breaking the Pakistani Shahid Afridi's 17-year record by one ball. In Test cricket, Viv Richards (West Indies) holds the record for the fastest Test century (56 balls); Nathan Astle (New Zealand) for the fastest double hundred (153 balls); with Virender Sehwag (India) the fastest to 300 (278 balls).

Test grounds in England and Wales

EDGBASTON (BIRMINGHAM)
Capacity: 25,000
Built: 1882
First Test: 1902 (England v Australia)
Fact: In 2004, England's Marcus Trescothick became the first batsman to score a hundred in each innings of an Edgbaston Test (v West Indies).

TRENT BRIDGE (NOTTINGHAM)
Capacity: 17,500
Built: 1841
First Test: 1899 (England v Australia)
Fact: The ground's most celebrated landmark, a 170-year-old elm tree named after former Notts cricketer George Parr, was destroyed during a gale in 1976.

SWALEC STADIUM (CARDIFF)
Capacity: 16,000
Built: 2008
First Test: 2009 (England v Australia)
Fact: Redevelopment of the old Sophia Gardens ground, headquarters of the Glamorgan County Cricket Club since 1967.

LORD'S (LONDON)
Capacity: 28,000
Built: 1814
First Test: 1884 (England v Australia)
Fact: The playing area drops 2.5 metres (8 feet) from north to south; the famous Lord's slope.

THE OVAL (LONDON)
Capacity: 23,500
Built: 1845
First Test: 1880 (England v Australia)
Fact: Sir Len Hutton scored a record 364 here against Australia in 1938.

ROSE BOWL (SOUTHAMPTON)
Capacity: 15,000
Built: 2001
First Test: 2011 (England v Sri Lanka)
Fact: Here in 2013 Australia's Aaron Finch set a new world record for Twenty20 internationals by scoring 156 runs off 63 balls (v England).

RIVERSIDE GROUND (CHESTER-LE-STREET)
Capacity: 17,000
Built: 1995
First Test: 2003 (England v Zimbabwe)
Fact: The ground's most distinctive feature is the fourteenth-century Lumley Castle, home to the Earls of Scarbrough, which overlooks it.

OLD TRAFFORD (MANCHESTER)
Capacity: 26,000
Built: 1857
First Test: 1884 (England v Australia)
Fact: The 1884 match, which was drawn, was the first official Ashes Test (though the fourteenth Test overall between the two countries).

HEADINGLEY (LEEDS)
Capacity: 20,000
Built: 1890
First Test: 1899 (England v Australia)
Fact: Yorkshire spinner Hedley Verity took 10 for 10 in a county match here in 1932, still the best bowling analysis in first-class cricket.

* Bramall Lane in Sheffield, built in 1855 and used as a ground by Yorkshire until 1973, staged one Test match (v Australia) in 1902.

CHAPTER 5

GREAT DOUBLE ACTS

With those two little pals of mine
Ramadhin and Valentine.
EGBERT MOORE ('VICTORY CALYPSO', LORD'S 1950)

Many of the best cricketers have prospered in pairs, their coupled names rolling off the tongue as familiarly as Morecambe and Wise. Greenidge and Haynes, Hayden and Langer, Strauss and Cook, among modern openers. Fast-bowling duos like Lindwall and Miller, Donald and Pollock, Ambrose and Walsh, Anderson and Broad. Spinners, for the most part, are more solitary predators. Laker and Lock wreaked havoc for Surrey on the county circuit in the 1950s, though they combined less successfully for England.

Here are five of the game's greatest double acts.

No master bowler

In 1909–10, Jack Hobbs (later Sir John Berry Hobbs) opened the bowling for England in three Tests against South Africa, taking one wicket – his only wicket in Test cricket. A lively medium-pace bowler in his younger days, he took 108 first-class wickets in all, which suggests he was wise to concentrate on his batting.

Hobbs and Sutcliffe

Jack Hobbs and Herbert Sutcliffe were, until Andrew Strauss and Alastair Cook overtook their record in 2010, the most prolific openers in Test history. What's more, they reached their total of 3,249 runs in less than half the number of innings it took the new record holders, with an average opening stand of 87.81.

Both batsmen had other regular partners. Hobbs, older by twelve years, opened for Surrey and England before the First World War with Tom Hayward, an early mentor. In 1907, they shared in four three-figure stands during the course of one week. Later, Hobbs regularly opened for England with Yorkshire's Wilfred Rhodes (who had made it all the way up from eleventh in the batting order), on one occasion the pair putting on 323 against Australia at Melbourne. Meanwhile, back at The Oval, Andy Sandham (the first batsman to score a Test triple century) had taken over as Hobbs' long-term county partner.

Sutcliffe's own regular opening partner at Yorkshire was Percy Holmes. Against Essex, at Leyton in 1932, the two of them put on 555 for the first wicket, for 45 years a world record. On ten other occasions they shared stands of 250 or more. But it was his seven-year Test partnership with Hobbs that captivated the cricketing public and turned the pair into household names.

Hobbs and Sutcliffe opened for England thirty-eight times. Their first joint appearance in a Test was at Edgbaston against South Africa in 1924. Hobbs was aged 42, Sutcliffe 30. Together they put on 136 runs, the first of 15 opening stands of over 100. They carried on in Australia that winter, with partnerships of 157, 110 and 283 in successive Test innings. In the Melbourne Test they batted throughout the third day – the first such instance in a Test match. Sutcliffe became the first batsman to make a hundred in each innings of a Test against Australia and the first Englishman to score three successive Test centuries. Eighteen months later Hobbs became the first batsman to pass 4,000 runs in Test cricket.

Between them, this remarkable duo notched 346 first-class centuries (Hobbs 197, Sutcliffe 149). Hobbs, who scored his last Test hundred at the age of 46, was dubbed 'The Master'. But Herbert Sutcliffe wasn't far behind.

Edrich and Compton

The 'Middlesex Twins' (usually three and four in the batting order) brought much-needed excitement and entertainment to austerity-ridden post-war Britain. Bill Edrich, who had won the Distinguished Flying Cross as a squadron leader in RAF Bomber Command, was a short, pugnacious batsman who would hook the fiercest bowling from in front of his nose. Denis Compton personified glamour, combining carefree good looks (his normally unruly hair slicked down with Brylcreem in a long-running advertising campaign) with an engagingly cavalier approach to the game that made light of his brilliant batting technique. Both could bowl: Edrich explosively and often erratically fast; Compton left-arm unorthodox spin. But it was their spectacular deeds with the bat that caught the eye – and almost invariably the opposition bowling attack.

Both had made England debuts before the war, but it was after the cessation of hostilities that they really came into their own. Nineteen forty-seven was their annus mirabilis. Compton headed the national batting averages with 3,816 runs at 90.85. Edrich came next with 3,539 runs at 80.43. Compton scored a record 18 centuries; Edrich 12. South Africa was the touring side that year, competing in a five-Test series. This time Edrich topped the averages with 552 runs (110.40) and a highest innings of 191. Compton totalled 753 runs (94.12) with a top score of 208. It was a long, hot summer, not least for fielding sides when Edrich and Compton were at the crease.

The Middlesex pair continued to clock up plenty of runs for their county and country in the following years, but never again reached the zenith of 1947. Compton, who played football for Arsenal and for England in 14 wartime internationals, was increasingly troubled by a recurring knee injury, which eventually shortened his career. But not before he and his batting partner had one more claim to glory. At The Oval in 1953, England regained the Ashes after 18 years and 362 days. In front of a delirious crowd, Compton hit the winning runs off part-time bowler Arthur Morris. Backing up at the other end was Bill Edrich.

Ramadhin and Valentine

In 1950, West Indies visited England for the first time in 11 years. There were several new faces in the squad, including two young spinners, Sonny Ramadhin (21) and Alf Valentine (20). Both were surprise selections in a side that had a strong batting line-up but was underpowered in the pace department. Little was known about either bowler, since they had played only two first-class matches apiece (the pre-selection trial games) before making the tour.

Ramadhin, the first East Indian to represent West Indies, was a short, neat figure who wore his sleeves buttoned at the wrist and often bowled wearing a cap. He bowled right-arm off-breaks and leg-breaks with no discernible change of action, using fingers rather than wrist to spin the ball. The taller Valentine bowled left-arm spin of immaculate length, vigorously tweaking the ball to achieve maximum turn. Halfway through the tour it was discovered that he couldn't read the scoreboard from the wicket, after which he was prescribed a pair of NHS glasses that he wore thereafter.

England comfortably won the first Test at Old Trafford, though Valentine's 8 for 104 in the first innings (11 wickets in the match) was a sign of things to come. And they weren't long coming. The next match at Lord's made cricket history, West Indies achieving their first-ever Test victory in England by a whopping 326 runs. The home side (with the honourable exception of Cyril Washbrook who made a second-innings hundred) had few answers to the perplexing spin of Ramadhin and Valentine, who took 18 wickets between them. It inspired Egbert Moore (better known as 'Lord Beginner') to write his famous calypso – 'Victory Calypso' also known as 'Cricket, Lovely Cricket' – with its chorus rhythmically commemorating the spinning duo. And soon there was more to celebrate with West Indies going on to win the next two Tests and the series 3–1. Valentine finished with 33 wickets (20.42) in the rubber, Ramadhin with 26 (23.23). An otherwise feeble attack resulted in each of them bowling more than a thousand overs during the tour.

Seven years later England exacted a cruel revenge. In the first Test at Edgbaston, after Ramadhin (7 for 49 and without his spinning partner) had bowled West Indies into a strong position, a record second-innings stand of 411 between Peter May (285 not out) and Colin Cowdrey (154) finally turned the tables. But nobody wrote a calypso about them!

Lillee and Marsh

Dennis Lillee's name is more often than not coupled with that of Jeff Thomson. They were the most feared bowling combination of their time, in the 1970s destroying first England then West Indies with their blistering attack. But Lillee's partnership with Australian wicketkeeper Rodney Marsh was no less decisive and even more enduring. Together they made 'caught Marsh bowled Lillee' the best-known catchphrase in the game, clocking up a record 95 such dismissals in Test cricket alone.

Both had a belligerent approach on the field. Lillee never concealed his dislike (bordering on contempt) for batsmen, his aggression often spilling over into verbal abuse. But great bowling actions speak louder than words, and in his prime Lillee's positively roared. His bouncer was full of venom and his deadly outswinger fed a constant stream of catches to the predatory Marsh and the slip cordon alongside him. As time went on he sacrificed some of his speed for line and length and movement off the pitch, becoming an even more prolific wicket-taker in the process.

Rodney Marsh's first Test appearance might well have been his last. Chosen more for his batting than his wicketkeeping skills, he was jeeringly dubbed 'Irongloves' by the crowd because of his fumbling of the ball. But, like many a cricketer before him who had made an unpromising start to a Test career, Marsh overcame this initial setback by working at his technique. The selectors wisely persevered with the burly, pugnacious Western Australian and before long he had become one of the most influential members of the team. He was behind the stumps for practically every ball that Lillee bowled in Test cricket, spectacularly pulling off catch after catch at full stretch.

It was fitting that both men should bow out of Test cricket at the same time – at Sydney in January 1984, in the fifth Test against Pakistan. In one of those statistical quirks with which the history of cricket abounds, both finished with exactly the same record number of dismissals: 355. Typically, Lillee had the last word, taking a wicket with his final ball.

Mistaken identity

In June 1981, many sports followers were shocked to learn that the cricketer Alec Bedser, twin brother of Eric, had been killed in a car accident in Transvaal. It soon became clear, however, that it was not the great Surrey and England bowler who had died but a South African namesake. Alec and Eric Bedser, born in East London, Cape Province, in 1948, were named after the famous Surrey twins. Both grew up to become more than competent cricketers. Alec, right-hand bat and medium-pace bowler, played three times for Border in the Currie Cup, and Eric was a consistent performer at senior club level.

Wasim Akram and Waqar Younis

Not every great partnership is harmoniously forged. The acrimonious spats between Wasim Akram and Waqar Younis disrupted an already volatile Pakistan dressing room. According to some of their teammates the two men were often on non-speaking terms, even on the field, with Inzamam-ul-Haq and others acting as go-betweens. Yet, they combined to create one of the most destructive bowling attacks in the modern game, competitively egged on by each other's success.

Wasim, one of the best left-arm fast bowlers the game has ever seen, was a master of swing and seam, backed up when required by a deadly bouncer or a skilfully concealed slower delivery. He made his Test debut against New Zealand in 1985 and by the time he had finished 17 years later, his tally of Test wickets stood at 414, to which can be added his 502 ODI scalps. As a batsman, given his unquestionable talent, he might be said to have under-delivered, despite a monumental knock of 257 not out against Zimbabwe in 1996.

Waqar joined his fellow Punjabi in the Pakistan side four years later, taking four wickets in India's first innings, including that of another debutant, Sachin Tendulkar, whom he cleaned bowled for 15. Despite his scorching pace, the climax of a surging approach to the wicket, Waqar rarely resorted to short-pitched bowling. His stock delivery was fast and full, with a lethal late inswing designed to hit the base of the stumps or the batsman's toes, and sometimes managing to strike both. Even more damagingly, he perfected the technique of reverse swing. His international span was in tandem with Wasim's, though because of injury he played fewer matches overall. His wicket tally was nevertheless impressive: 373 Test dismissals, 416 in ODIs.

Wasim and Waqar troubled the very best batsmen around the world. When the two of them were on song (even if they weren't singing from the same song sheet) there was no relief to be found at either end. Statistically, they were neck and neck. Wasim took five wickets in a Test innings on 25 occasions; Waqar achieved the feat 22 times. Both registered seven-wicket hauls as their best Test performance. So much in common, yet so little common ground.

CHAPTER 6

THE WOMEN'S GAME

I was twelve before I realised there was such a thing as women's cricket.

CHARLOTTE EDWARDS (ENGLAND CAPTAIN)

On 26 July 1745, a year before the Battle of Culloden, the *Reading Mercury* reported on a cricket match between 'eleven maids of Bramley and eleven maids of Hambleton'. The Hambleton maids came out on top by eight 'notches'. It is the first known account of the female side of the game.

It was not until 1887 however that the first women's cricket club was founded, at Nun Appleton in Yorkshire. Three years later 'The Original English Lady Cricketers' were divided into a Red XI and a Blue XI and played a number of exhibition games around the country. Their on-field strip was a white flannel blouse and long skirt, colour coded around the collar and hem and by a sash around the waist. In 1926, the Women's Cricket Association was formed in England, and official organisations were established in Australia (1931) and New Zealand (1933). Other cricket-playing nations gradually followed suit after the war.

The first women's Test match took place between Australia and England at Brisbane in December 1934. It was first blood to England, who also won the second Test at Sydney and the three-match series 2–0. England's player of the series was Myrtle Maclagan, who took 7 for 10 with her off-breaks in Australia's inaugural innings (a record which stood until 1958). In the second match she became the first female Test centurion. The success of the women's team was in marked contrast to the fortunes of the men's side, which in England a few months before had surrendered the Ashes, prompting the *Morning Post* newspaper to publish the following quatrain:

> *What matter that we lost, mere nervy men*
> *Since England's women now play England's game,*
> *Wherefore Immortal* Wisden, *take your pen*
> *And write MACLAGAN on the scroll of fame.*

Australia toured England for the first time in 1937. It was a tight series, with one match apiece and the final Test drawn. England's Betty Snowball became the first woman to be run out for 99 in a Test match. Until 1960, these two countries, along with New Zealand, were the only Test-playing nations.

Inevitably, the ongoing tussle between England and Australia has been the principal focus, with the initiative swinging from one hemisphere to the other. Of the 19 series played between the two countries to date, Australia has won seven, England five and seven have been drawn. When England came out on top in 2005, it was their first series victory over the old enemy for 42 years.

In 1998, what had always been unofficially understood became official: the two countries would now compete for the Ashes Trophy, and unlike the men's version there was to be no doubt as to what the incinerated remains were. At a formal ceremony at Lord's a miniature bat, signed by the England and Australian teams, and a copy of the WCA Constitution and Rules Book were consigned to the flames. A trophy made of wood from an ancient yew tree is the Ashes' sealed resting place.

In 2013, for the first time, the Ashes series was contested across all three formats of the game on the basis of a points system: the single Test counting for six points; the three ODIs two points each; and the three Twenty20 games a further two points apiece. The Test match was drawn but England regained the Ashes, lost two years earlier, on the strength of a convincing 5–1 victory in the shorter formats.

World Cups

The first women's ODI World Cup was staged in England in 1973, beating the men to a tournament by two years. With not enough countries to go round, an 'International XI' competed to make up the numbers. It was a round-robin format with England and Australia playing the last scheduled match, which in effect became the final. The home side won. In the nine World Cup tournaments since then, Australia has lifted the trophy six times, England twice. New Zealand, on home ground in 2000, has been the only exception to the rule.

England were champions in the first ICC Women's Twenty20 World Cup, defeating New Zealand in the final at Lord's in 2009, pace bowler Katherine Brunt taking a match-winning 3 for 6. The 2010 and 2012 tournaments were won by Australia.

Myrtle Maclagan (England)

In her 14-Test career (1934–51) Myrtle Maclagan scored just over 1,000 runs and took 60 wickets. She regularly opened the batting with Betty Snowball, the media dubbing them the Hobbs and Sutcliffe of women's cricket. Her bowling was a versatile mix of seam and off-spin.

Betty Wilson (Australia)

The first cricketer of either sex to make a century and take ten wickets in the same Test. It happened at Melbourne against England in 1958. Wilson scored exactly 100 in Australia's second innings and with the ball took 7 for 7 and 4 for 9, giving her the astonishing match figures of 11 for 16 – which included the first women's Test hat-trick.

Enid Bakewell (England)

Bakewell scored a century on her debut in 1968 – against Australia – the first of four she made in 12 Tests. She scored a half-century in each innings of a Test on four occasions, and was the first to register back-to-back hundreds. No less effective with the ball, her left-arm spin harvested 50 Test wickets at an economical 16 runs apiece.

Rachael Heyhoe-Flint (England)

In an international career spanning two decades, Rachael Heyhoe-Flint won 22 Test caps and played in 23 ODIs. During the 11 years in which she captained England in Tests (1966–77), the side remained undefeated. She was the first woman to hit a six in a Test match, and led her country to victory in the inaugural World Cup in 1973.

Diana Edulji (India)

The Mumbai-born Diana Edulji played in India's first Test match, against West Indies at Bangalore in 1976. A very effective left-arm orthodox spinner, she took 63 Test wickets and a further 46 in ODIs. She captained her country in both formats of the game and for the best part of 17 years was India's most outstanding woman cricketer.

Belinda Clark (Australia)

Clark held the Australian record for the most runs both in Test matches (919) and ODIs (4,844), averaging over 45 in each format. Her 118 ODI appearances was another record. Thirteen years before Sachin Tendulkar emulated the feat, she scored a double century in a one-day international (229 not out against Denmark in 1997). She captained Australia to victory in the 1997 and 2005 World Cups.

Jan Brittin (England)

The Surrey right-hander set new records in both the long and short forms of the game. She scored ten centuries in her 27 Tests and 63 ODIs (five in each format). In 1984, she became the first woman cricketer to score over 500 runs in a calendar year; and in 1998 made back-to-back Test hundreds against Australia, including a career-best 167.

Emily Drumm (New Zealand)

Emily Drumm made her Test debut at the age of 17. She played five Tests in all, scoring two centuries and two fifties in six innings and finishing with an average of 144.33. She appeared in 101 ODIs, captaining her country in 41 of them. Her greatest triumph was leading New Zealand to victory in the 2000 World Cup.

Claire Taylor (England)

An outstanding performer with the bat, Taylor scored centuries in consecutive Tests against South Africa in 2003 (177 and 131). Three years later in a one-day international against India at Lord's she made 156, one of a record eight hundreds in ODIs. In 2009, she became the first woman to be listed as one of *Wisden's* Five Cricketers of the Year.

Mithali Raj (India)

In only her third Test, against England at Taunton in 2002, the 19-year-old Mithali Raj scored a record 214. She is by far her country's most prolific run-getter in ODIs, and fourth highest in the international rankings. In 2005, she led India to their first World Cup final, and a year later to their first-ever Test series win in England.

Cathryn Fitzpatrick (Australia)

At around 120 kph (75 mph), Cathryn Fitzpatrick was the world's fastest female bowler. Her disconcerting pace helped Australia to victory in the 1997 and 2005 World Cups, and her career haul of 180 wickets in ODIs (average 16.79) remains a world record. She took a further 60 wickets in her 13 Test appearances, the last of them against India in 2006.

Charlotte Edwards (England)

England's charismatic captain has led from the front, scoring four centuries to date in Test matches and twice that number in ODIs. To add to that are the 60-plus wickets she has captured with her leg-breaks. In 2009, she led England to victory in both the World Cup and ICC Twenty20, and captained the side that triumphantly regained the Ashes in 2013.

CRICKET CENTRE STAGE

All was peace till I bungled that catch.

P. G. WODEHOUSE ('MISSED')

There has always been a strong bond between the worlds of cricket and theatre, the on-field drama seemingly resonating with that on stage. The Scottish dramatist J. M. Barrie, creator of Peter Pan, founded his own cricket team, the Allahakbarries. Arthur Conan Doyle, P. G. Wodehouse and A. A. Milne were among the writers who regularly turned out for Barrie's distinctly literary side. Not all of them took these Edwardian escapades on the cricket field seriously, though Conan Doyle was an accomplished club cricketer and once when playing for MCC clean bowled W. G. Grace – but not before the great man had scored 110. This prize wicket was Conan Doyle's only scalp in first-class cricket and prompted him to write a celebratory 19-verse poem on the subject.

P. G. Wodehouse represented his school, Dulwich College, as a medium-fast bowler. Until he took up permanent residency in America, the affable 'Plum' was an enthusiastic follower of the game.

He famously named the immortal Jeeves after a Warwickshire cricketer killed at the Battle of the Somme. The Yorkshire-born Percy Jeeves was a promising all-rounder for his adopted county Warwickshire, good enough to be selected for the Players against the Gentlemen in 1914 and who but for the war might well have gone on to win an England cap.

Another man of the theatre and once a keen cricketer was the Irish avant-garde playwright and novelist Samuel Beckett, author of *Waiting for Godot*. Beckett, who was awarded the Nobel Prize in Literature in 1969, spent most of his adult life in Paris and moved in circles far removed from cricket. Yet, the writer never lost his interest in the game, forged when he was a schoolboy in Dublin. A left-hand opening bat and medium-pace bowler, he played two first-class games for Dublin University against Northamptonshire in the 1920s but with little success (his highest score in four innings was 18 and he failed to take a wicket). It was enough though to get a mention in *Wisden* (the only Nobel Laureate to have achieved this distinction), an acknowledgement that both amused and delighted Beckett.

Harold Pinter, who as a playwright was greatly influenced by Samuel Beckett, never played first-class cricket. For many years however he was the leading light of the Gaieties Cricket Club (founded in 1937 by the music hall artist, Lupino Lane), first as a player, then as captain, and finally as chairman. Despite his London East End upbringing Pinter was a lifetime supporter of Yorkshire CCC. Cricket metaphors and references abound in his work: two films for which he wrote screenplays – *Accident* and *The Go-Between* – feature cricket matches, but the biggest clue to the writer's lifelong love of the game comes in his play, *No Man's Land*. Each of the four characters in the play (referred to by their surnames only) shares the name of a famous England cricketer of the so-called 'Golden Age': Hirst (George), Spooner (Reginald), Briggs (Johnny) and Foster (Frank of Warwickshire, a fine all-rounder and no relation of the seven Worcestershire Fosters), though the dramatic work itself has nothing whatsoever to do with the sport.

Cricketing inspiration

The father of the writer H. G. Wells was the first cricketer to take four wickets in four balls in a first-class match. Joseph Wells, a Kent professional who bowled round-arm at pace, performed the feat for his county against Sussex at Brighton in 1862. His son, whose fame was to outstrip that of his father, always professed to have no interest in cricket. Is it then simply a coincidence that the eponymous hero of one of his most celebrated novels, Kipps, shares the name of a well-known eighteenth century Kent cricketer?

The Final Test

Terence Rattigan, whose hugely popular plays include *The Browning Version*, *Separate Tables* and *The Deep Blue Sea*, transferred his love of cricket onto the big screen. Rattigan had been a talented schoolboy cricketer, opening the innings for Harrow against Eton in the annual fixture at Lord's in 1929 and scoring a solid 29. His school report at cricket was succinctly expressed: 'He has played many fine innings. His off-side strokes are masterful, especially those behind point. His bowling has lost a lot of the accuracy it had last year. His fielding at slip has been excellent.'

The Final Test began life as a television play before being adapted for the cinema in 1953. Veteran England batsman Sam Palmer (played by Jack Warner) is about to make his last Test appearance, against Australia at The Oval, after a long and successful career. Interwoven with the build-up to this momentous event are a characteristic Rattigan father-son relationship and a romantic sub-plot. Newsreel footage of England v Australia at The Oval helps create an authentic atmosphere, as do the somewhat self-conscious walk-on roles of Sam Palmer's teammates, the real-life Len Hutton, Denis Compton, Alec Bedser, Jim Laker, Cyril Washbrook and Godfrey Evans.

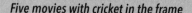

Five movies with cricket in the frame

P'tang, Yang, Kipperbang (1982)
Coming-of-age story about a cricket-obsessed schoolboy.

Playing Away (1987)
Comedy about an English village club that stages a Third World cricket week.

Iqbal (2005)
A Bollywood story about a deaf-mute boy who dreams of playing cricket for India.

Hit for Six (2007)
Barbadian drama about match-fixing and featuring several famous West Indian cricketers.

Hansie (2008)
The decline and fall of South Africa's disgraced captain, Hansie Cronje.

Cricket – the musical

Having not worked together since the successful launch of their musical *Evita* in 1978, Tim Rice and his collaborator Andrew Lloyd Webber were commissioned by Prince Edward to write a show for the Queen's sixtieth birthday. A self-confessed cricket addict with his own team, The Heartaches (the club's motto, *Clava recta*, means 'a straight bat'), Rice leapt at the chance of producing something on the theme of his favourite sport.

The result of their revived partnership was a 25-minute mini-musical entitled *Cricket*, first performed at Windsor Castle on 18 June 1986. Trevor Nunn directed the production, which light-heartedly tells the story of a young cricketer forced to make a choice between the demands of his girlfriend and the requirements of his team. Most of the characters have spoof names that are cricket-related: Donald Hobbs, the Earl of Headingley and his daughter Emma Kirkstall-Lane, and a West Indian fast bowler named Winston B. Packer. There is no spoken dialogue and among the show's 11 songs are 'The Summer Game', 'The Art of Bowling', 'The Final Stand' and the concluding number 'One Hot Afternoon'. *Cricket*, graciously received on the night, was staged only twice more and Lloyd Webber went on to use several of the tunes in his later musical *Aspects of Love*.

Away days

Actor Trevor Howard who played a starring role in such films as Brief Encounter, The Third Man, Ryan's Daughter *and* The Charge of the Light Brigade, *had a standard clause in his contract excusing him from work during a Test match at Lord's.*

Battle cry

During the interval at the second ODI between New Zealand and England at Wellington in 2002, film director Peter Jackson, microphone in hand, conducted a responsive crowd of 30,000 cricket fans in a series of howling, growling and grunting noises. The recorded sound effects were for a battle scene in The Two Towers, *the second film in his* Lord of the Rings *trilogy. The home side went on to win the match by 155 runs, giving the crowd something else to shout about.*

All-star XI

The Hollywood Cricket Club was founded in 1932 by the English stage and screen actor Charles Aubrey Smith. Smith's other claim to fame was as a cricketer, having captained England to victory in his only Test match – against South Africa at Port Elizabeth in 1889, the first international encounter between the two countries. Known as 'Round the Corner' Smith because of his oddly curved run-up as a bowler (W. G. Grace once remarked, 'It is rather startling when he suddenly appears at the bowling crease'), he won a cricket Blue at Cambridge and went on to play for Sussex for the next 14 years. In his solitary Test appearance he took seven wickets with his right-arm medium pace, including 5 for 19 in South Africa's first innings.

Essentially Sunday cricketers, the Hollywood club took itself seriously enough to have its own predictably flamboyant uniform: a blazer with magenta, mauve and black stripes, and a harlequin-style cap. Errol Flynn (Tasmanian by birth), Laurence Olivier, Boris Karloff (real name William Pratt and a lifetime supporter of Surrey) who kept wicket, David Niven and the Sherlock Holmes/Dr Watson duo of Basil Rathbone and Nigel Bruce, were among the ex-pat cricketers of variable talent who turned out for the celebrity team. P. G. Wodehouse was the club's first secretary.

As a subtle nod to his cricketing past, C. Aubrey Smith (as he was known on screen) named his Beverly Hills home 'The Round Corner'. He was knighted in 1944 for his contribution to Anglo-American friendship.

The Lord's Taverners

Cricket's best-known charity is The Lord's Taverners, formed in 1950 by a handful of actors who used to congregate at the old tavern at Lord's Cricket Ground. Early members of the club included Richard Attenborough, Jack Hawkins and the broadcaster John Snagge. John Mills was the first president and the Duke of Edinburgh agreed to be 'Patron and Twelfth Man' – a dual role he has performed ever since. Fund-raising matches were arranged with showbiz personalities playing alongside their cricketing heroes, who in turn were delighted to rub shoulders with stars of stage and screen. Sixty years on The Lord's Taverners is still going strong, having raised millions of pounds to help disabled children and to promote cricket in deprived inner-city areas of the UK.

Hail Caesar!

One of the most unlikely names to have featured in first-class cricket is Julius Caesar. In the middle of the nineteenth century a cricketer of that name (and it was his real one) was for many years a key member of the Surrey side. A short, powerfully built man, Caesar was an accomplished batsman and brilliant outfielder who went on the first overseas tours to North America and Australia. Off the field he was said to be an entertaining character who would enliven the dressing room with his merry quips – not something his illustrious namesake was famous for.

CHAPTER 8

AGE MATTERS

Cricket is not like a government job where retirement age is fixed at sixty. A cricketer can retire at thirty or sixty; it's up to the player.

VIRENDER SEHWAG (INDIA)

Late starters and finishers

The oldest cricketer to make his Test debut was James Southerton, who was 49 years 119 days when he played for England in the inaugural match at Melbourne in 1877. Three years later he became the first Test cricketer to die, falling ill with pleurisy. Since Test matches were not officially designated as such until much later, the significance of his early demise escaped the unfortunate Southerton.

An off-break bowler, who switched from round-arm to over-arm, Southerton played for Surrey, Sussex and Hampshire – sometimes, in the days before birth and residential qualifications, in the same season. Although he was 32 before he took a wicket in first-class cricket, his seasonal tally exceeded a hundred wickets on ten occasions. In 1869, in a match against Lancashire, he became the first bowler to take four wickets in five balls.

Once, when batting, he believed that he was caught and 'walked'. The fielding side sportingly insisted that the catch had not been made but Southerton refused to change his mind. His dismissal was recorded in the scorebook:

J. Southerton, retired, thinking he was caught, 0

The great Yorkshire all-rounder Wilfred Rhodes is the oldest cricketer to have played in a Test match. He was 52 years 165 days when in 1930 he made the last of his 58 Test appearances for England. Rhodes also holds the record for the longest Test career, just short of 31 years, during which time he scored 2,325 runs and captured 127 wickets.

Having seemingly retired from Test cricket, Rhodes had been recalled to the England side in 1926 for the final match against Australia at The Oval, aged 48. The previous four Tests had been drawn and with all to play for England appointed A. P. F. ('Percy') Chapman as its new captain. (When Rhodes made his Test debut in 1898, Chapman had not yet been born.) Set to score over four hundred runs to win, Australia collapsed in their second innings and were all out for 125. Rhodes with his slow left-arm spin (4 for 44) did most of the damage. England won by 289 runs and regained the Ashes.

Playing in the same match, and scoring his only Test hundred against Australia on his home ground, was Jack Hobbs. The Surrey batsman was another with a long and glittering career. He was 42 years old when he overtook W. G. Grace's record of 126 first-class centuries, reaching the milestone against Somerset at Taunton in August 1925. He went on to make a further 71 three-figure scores before retiring at the age of 51. His career total of 197 centuries is unlikely to be beaten.

The oldest Australian to play Test cricket (and the second oldest overall) was Bert Ironmonger, a left-arm spinner whose bowling action was considered questionable in some quarters. As a child he had lost the top joint of his forefinger in a chaff-cutter on the family farm and learned to spin the ball off the remaining stump. A less than agile, thick-set figure, nicknamed 'Dainty' by his teammates, Ironmonger was a liability in the field but a very effective wicket-taker, his 74 Test dismissals costing less than 18 runs apiece. He made his first Test appearance in 1928 at the age of 46 (he claimed to be 41 at the time) and his last a month short of his 51st birthday. His prowess with the ball was not matched by his batsmanship. The story goes that on one occasion his wife telephoned him at the Melbourne ground only to be told that he had just gone in to bat. 'Don't worry,' she replied, 'I'll hang on.'

Among leading contemporary cricketers, Sachin Tendulkar was in his 41st year when he retired in 2013 and (at the time of writing) Misbah-ul-Haq, Shivnarine Chanderpaul and Jacques Kallis are all pushing 40 while still active in the game. The Indian Premier League has provided some top players with a lucrative coda to their careers, but the demands of modern professional cricket, not least in the fielding department, dictate that players generally retire much earlier than those of former times.

Late starter

In 1950, at the age of 72, Raja Sir Maharaj Singh, captaining the Bombay Governor's XI in a three-day match against a touring Commonwealth XI, became the oldest cricketer to make his first-class debut and the oldest to play in any first-class match. In his one innings, batting at number nine, he was dismissed for four runs off the bowling of Jim Laker. The age difference between batsman and bowler was a trifling 44 years. After his brief appearance on the opening day – the extent of his first-class career – Singh played no further part in the game, handing over the captaincy to the younger and even more grandly titled Maharaja of Patiala, a veteran of 50 first-class matches, including one Test cap.

Young beginners

The youngest Test debutant on record is Pakistan's Hasan Raza, who was allegedly 14 years 227 days when he appeared against Zimbabwe at Faisalabad in October 1996. Subsequent doubts were raised about his date of birth, leaving some uncertainty as to his exact age at the time, which is now thought to have been closer to 15. Coming in at number five the precocious young batsman scored a respectable 27 in his one innings in the match. Despite an impressive record in domestic cricket the gifted Hasan Raza played in only seven Tests, with a top score of 68.

Fellow countryman Mushtaq Mohammad was said to be 15 when he won his first Test cap in 1959, though his date of birth remains unconfirmed as well. What is not in doubt is his quality as a player. One of five brothers who played first-class cricket (four of them at Test level) Mushtaq was an outstanding all-rounder, a fine batsman with 72 first-class hundreds to his name and one of the world's best leg-spinners. He captained his country 19 times during the seventies and played several seasons for Northamptonshire, leading them to their first major trophy, the Gillette Cup, in 1976.

Most of the fifty youngest Test cricketers on record herald from the Indian subcontinent, those from Bangladesh joining the ranks of Indian and Pakistani. Sachin Tendulkar was only 16 when he made his Test debut in 1989, losing his wicket to Waqar Younis who was little more than a year older. Cricketers from other parts of the world generally take longer to mature, or at any rate to make it into the Test arena. Among the rare exceptions have been West Indies' Garry Sobers and Australia's Ian Craig, both only 17 when they first represented their countries in the fifties, and New Zealand's Daniel Vettori who was 18.

England's youngest capped player remains, after more than sixty years, Yorkshire's Brian Close. Chosen for the third Test against New Zealand in 1949 at the age of 18 years 149 days, he made an inauspicious start. Selected as an all-rounder (he batted left-handed and bowled right, medium pace as well as off-spin), he failed to score in his only innings and took just one wicket in the match. Taken on tour to Australia the following year, he made 0 and 1 in his only Test. Thereafter, Close made only sporadic appearances for England, though he proved to be an outstanding cricketer at county level. He captained Yorkshire and later Somerset with great success, always leading by example.

In 1966 he was appointed captain of England, but the use of blatant delaying tactics in a county match against Warwickshire cost him the job. He made his last Test appearance in 1976 at the age of 45. It was 27 years since he had first donned an England cap; in terms of longevity, second only to Wilfred Rhodes.

Youngest Test debuts by country

England
Brian Close (1949),
all-rounder,
18 years 149 days

West Indies
Derek Sealy (1930),
batsman,
17 years 122 days

Zimbabwe
Hamilton Masakadza (2001),
batsman,
17 years 254 days

South Africa
Paul Adams (1995),
left-arm chinaman,
18 years 340 days

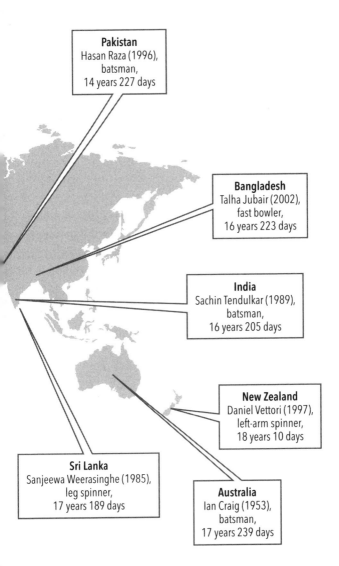

Pakistan
Hasan Raza (1996),
batsman,
14 years 227 days

Bangladesh
Talha Jubair (2002),
fast bowler,
16 years 223 days

India
Sachin Tendulkar (1989),
batsman,
16 years 205 days

New Zealand
Daniel Vettori (1997),
left-arm spinner,
18 years 10 days

Sri Lanka
Sanjeewa Weerasinghe (1985),
leg spinner,
17 years 189 days

Australia
Ian Craig (1953),
batsman,
17 years 239 days

Younger than Young

Selected for Yorkshire against Durham MCCU in 2011 at the age of 15 years 27 days, wicketkeeper Barney Gibson became the youngest-ever cricketer to play in an English first-class game. He beat the record established in 1867 by Charles Young of Hampshire, who was 104 days older when he made his debut. At the time, the teenage Gibson was a pupil at Crawshaw School in Pudsey, birthplace of Yorkshire legends Herbert Sutcliffe and Sir Leonard Hutton. He pouched six catches in the match, one of them a spectacular effort down the legside, and then went back to school.

Record career

Athanasios John Traicos is the only Egyptian-born Test cricketer. He grew up in South Africa and developed into a fine off-spinner, selected to play for his country in the 1969–70 series against Australia – the last before South Africa was cast into the sporting wilderness. His three-match Test career appeared to be at an end but in 1992, at the age of 45, he was selected to play for Zimbabwe, who had recently been granted Test status. In the inaugural match against India at Harare, Traicos was Zimbabwe's most successful bowler with 5 for 86 in 50 overs. The interval of 22 years and 222 days between his Test appearances established a world record that still stands.

CHAPTER 9

CRICKET IS A FUNNY GAME

I don't wish to denigrate a sport that is enjoyed by millions, some of them awake and facing the right way, but it is an odd game.
BILL BRYSON (*DOWN UNDER*)

Cricket when played seriously is no laughing matter, except perhaps to those who don't understand it. But it is by and large a good-humoured game, one that has often attracted eccentric characters – on and off the field – and cultivated the bizarre. No other sport delights so much in its oddities.

Cricket at sea

Few cricket matches are over as quickly as the annual Bramble Bank fixture. Staged once a year on a sandbank in the middle of the Solent – usually late August or early September at low tide, when the venue briefly surfaces – the game generally lasts no more than an hour, after which the sea reasserts itself. Teams, and their supporters, from the Royal Southern Yacht Club at Hamble and the Island Sailing Club on the Isle of Wight arrive at the 'ground' in a flotilla of boats, the players wearing full cricket regalia.

Speed is of the essence. Depending on how much the sea has receded, batsmen and bowlers can be above their ankles in water, with fieldsmen in the deep just that. It's not the winning that's important but the taking part. There isn't time for a tea interval – after all, who wants soggy sandwiches? – just a big slap-up dinner when everyone has dried off.

High achiever

In 1899, Arthur Collins, a 13-year-old pupil at Clifton College in Bristol, scored 628 not out in a college house match. The highest individual score in recorded cricket, his innings lasted 6 hours, 50 minutes and was spread over four afternoons, some of them interrupted by rain. Opening the innings for Clarke's House against North Town, he carried his bat in a total of 836 all out. With number eleven 'Redfern' he added 183 for the last wicket, the latter's contribution a mere 13. Collins's knock included a six, four fives, 31 fours, 33 threes and 146 twos. The school scorebook reads: '628 – plus or minus 20, shall we say'. Collins went on to take 11 wickets in the match (7 for 33 and 4 for 30), almost single-handedly clinching victory for his side by an innings and 688 runs.

Umpires and their quirks

One of the white-capped Dickie Bird's nervous mannerisms when standing at the bowler's end was to stretch out his forearms, as if shooting his cuffs, before every ball.

West Indian Steve Bucknor was known as 'Slow Death Bucknor' because of his habit of ponderously nodding in advance of raising the dreaded finger.

David Shepherd would superstitiously hop onto one leg when the score reached 111 ('Nelson'), or any multiple of it, and not put both feet on the ground until the score had moved on.

Rheumatoid arthritis is the cause of New Zealander Billy Bowden's less-than-upright dismissal finger, though it can't be blamed for his exaggerated sweeping gesture to signal a four or the goalkeeper-style leap that denotes a six.

At stumps, the long-standing English umpire Alec Skelding, one of the game's great characters, would routinely say, 'And that concludes the entertainment for the day, gentlemen.'

Umpire's signals

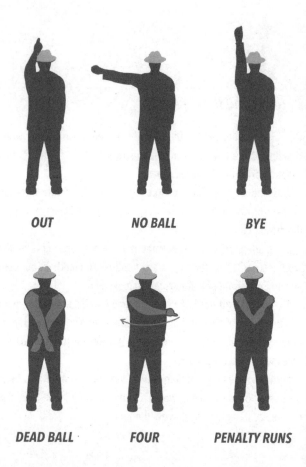

OUT   NO BALL   BYE

DEAD BALL   FOUR   PENALTY RUNS

BOUNDARY 6

NEW BALL

WIDE

LEG-BYE

SHORT RUN

CANCEL CALL

Tourist attraction

The Australian Aboriginal team that toured England in 1868 was the first overseas side to do so. During their five-month tour, the 13-man side played a total of 47 matches (14 wins, 14 defeats, 19 draws) kitted out in a distinctively patriotic uniform of red shirt, blue sash and white flannels. Their native names being beyond the grasp of the British public, most of the players were known by nicknames. When they were not engaged in playing cricket, Dick-a-Dick, Bullocky, Mosquito and others demonstrated their skills with boomerang and spear in front of enthusiastic crowds. Sadly, one of the party, King Cole, never made it home, dying of tuberculosis in a London hospital.

Jaw before wicket

Gloucestershire captain Tom Pugh was given out lbw in a county match against Northamptonshire in 1961, only it wasn't his leg in the path of the ball but his jaw. Ducking into a low full toss from England fast bowler David Larter, Pugh was struck on the side of the face plumb in front of the stumps. His jaw was broken in two places – and he hadn't even got off the mark!

Twenty20 retro

The first-ever international Twenty20 was played between New Zealand and Australia at Auckland in 2005. Staged largely as a fun event, both sides wore 1980s-style kit with the New Zealand team in the once familiar beige, now the uniform of their most fervent supporters, the 'Beige Brigade'. Some players sported moustaches, beards and hairstyles reminiscent of the eighties, competing for the best retro look. For the record, Australia won the match.

Fostershire

In the early years of the twentieth century seven Foster brothers played for Worcestershire, though only four turned out for the county (nicknamed 'Fostershire') at any one time. All seven were primarily batsmen, but the outstanding member of the brotherhood was R. E. ('Tip') Foster, who played eight times for England and scored a record 287 on his Test debut against Australia in 1903. He remains the only player to have captained England at both cricket and football.

Smokers v non-smokers

In 1887, a four-day match took place in Melbourne between adherents of the noxious weed and those who managed to live without it. The two sides were made up of members of Alfred Shaw's England XI, at the time touring Australia, and cricketers from the host country. Batting first, the Non-Smokers amassed a healthy 803, the highest total hitherto recorded in a first-class game, with England batsman Arthur Shrewsbury scoring 236. Despite the presence of several England players in their own line-up, the Smokers could only manage 356 and were forced to follow on. They were 135 for 5 in their second innings when the match finally ran out of puff.

Umpire's decision

In 1948, Glamorgan won the County Championship for the first time in the club's history. The Welsh side had been a late starter, not achieving first-class status until 1921, the 17th county to do so. Their championship moment of glory came on the third day of the match against Hampshire at Bournemouth. Having completely dominated the game throughout, Glamorgan had just one more wicket to take. The last Hampshire batsman was rapped on the pads and the umpire, former Glamorgan player Dai Davies, raised his finger and shouted: 'You're *out – and we've won!*'

Olympic cricket

Cricket has only once featured in the Olympic Games, at Paris in 1900. Only two nations competed – England and France (Belgium and the Netherlands having withdrawn) – with both countries represented by club sides. For England it was the Devon and Somerset Wanderers who took the field. The French side was largely made up of British ex-pats living in Paris. The two-day fixture took place in a deserted Vélodrome de Vincennes. England, comfortably the winners, received a silver medal, France a bronze. Some years later these were upgraded to gold and silver respectively, but cricket itself has stayed off the Olympic agenda.

CHAPTER 10

BRUISING ENCOUNTERS

Where else in the world do you get the opportunity to basically kill someone with two bouncers an over? Or try, legally.

DALE STEYN (SOUTH AFRICA)

Cricket is often light-heartedly portrayed as a placid, somewhat soporific sport, whose leisurely activity barely intrudes upon its dozing spectators. In reality of course, and especially at the highest level, the contest between bat and ball can be a brutally painful and physically damaging experience.

Here are some bruising encounters that left their mark:

Mind and body

Ellis Park in Johannesburg was the scene of one of the most wounding spells of fast bowling since the infamous Bodyline tour. It was the second Test between South Africa and New Zealand in 1953. The perpetrator was Neil

Adcock, tall, hostile and seriously quick, the first South African pace bowler to take 100 Test wickets. He clean bowled Murray Chapple and Matt Poore with thundering deliveries that first crashed into their unprotected chests. Then further short-pitched balls despatched two other batsmen to hospital, Lawrie Miller with a chest injury and Bert Sutcliffe with a head wound (helmets were still a couple of decades away).

The left-handed Sutcliffe, New Zealand's premier batsman and one of the finest in the world, returned with the score at 81 for 6. With his head heavily bandaged, he set about the South African bowlers in no uncertain style, hitting seven sixes and four fours in his 80 not out, made out of 106 in 112 minutes. It was fast scoring by most Test match standards, and exceptional for someone nursing a major headache. Last man in was fast bowler Bob Blair. As he made his way to the wicket the Johannesburg crowd stood in a silent mark of respect: the day before, Blair had learnt that his fiancée had been killed in the Tangiwai train disaster, his country's worst ever. In a partnership that lasted just ten minutes they put on 33 runs, 25 of them coming off a single (eight-ball) over from the great off-spinner, Hugh Tayfield. The pair's heroics were not enough to prevent New Zealand losing the match, but a tale of courage and defiance was born.

Brave face

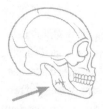

A fractured jaw is a rare injury in cricket. Even rarer is that someone should play with one. But that is exactly what happened during the fourth Test between West Indies and India at St John's, Antigua, in 2002. Indian leg-spinner Anil Kumble, the third highest wicket-taker in Test cricket and only the second bowler to have dismissed all ten batsmen in a Test innings, had sustained the injury when batting against West Indian pace man Mervyn Dillon. The next day, having been put on a liquid diet by the medics and with his jaw held in place by thick strapping that framed his face, Kumble was allowed to take the field for the final session. He bowled a spell of 14 consecutive overs (five of which were maidens) for just 29 runs and the prize wicket of Brian Lara, whom he trapped lbw for four.

Before flying back to India for immediate surgery, Kumble acknowledged that he had taken a risk in returning to the field, adding: 'At least I can now go home with the thought that I tried my best.' Nevertheless, with the high-scoring match (India 513 for 9 declared, West Indies 629 for 9 in reply) heading irrevocably for a draw, it is difficult to understand why the Indian management had taken such a gamble with their star bowler. In the event all 11 Indian players had a bowl – only the third time that this had happened in Test history. West Indies legend Viv Richards later said of Kumble's contribution: 'It was one of the bravest things I've seen on the field of play.'

Presidential encounter

The only US president to have watched Test cricket is Dwight D. Eisenhower, guest of honour on the fourth day of the third Test between Pakistan and Australia at Karachi in 1959. It is anyone's guess what the golf-loving ex-general made of the complex manoeuvres on the field, especially as it turned out to be one of the slowest-ever scoring days in Test history. Nearly fifty years later, President George W. Bush was given a brief demonstration of cricket on the lawn of the US embassy in Islamabad. The president faced three gentle deliveries from Inzamam-ul-Haq and bowled a couple himself. There is no record of him being dismissed 'lbdubya'.

In and out

 Andy Lloyd's Test career lasted 33 minutes. The left-handed Warwickshire opener, making his debut in the first Test against West Indies at Edgbaston in 1984, was struck on the temple (fortunately he was wearing a helmet) by a lifting ball from fast bowler Malcolm Marshall. It was the first morning of the match and England were 20 for 2, Lloyd's opening partner Graeme Fowler and Derek Randall both having been dismissed for a duck. Lloyd, who had scored ten, was swiftly taken to hospital and kept in for a week suffering from blurred vision. He played no further cricket that season.

Prior to his fleeting appearance in the Test match Lloyd had opened for England in all three ODIs against the tourists, top-scoring in two of them; but this would prove the sum total of his international career. He was never selected for England again, despite making a successful return to county cricket the following year and continuing to pile up the runs for Warwickshire until his retirement from the game in 1992. England lost the Edgbaston match by a humbling innings and 180 runs, but Andy Lloyd had the consolation of being the only Test opener never to have been dismissed.

Crunch time

A sickening on-field collision on the second day of the first Test against Sri Lanka at Kandy in 1999, left Australians Steve Waugh and Jason Gillespie with horrific injuries. Both fielders were attempting to catch a top edge from batsman Mahela Jayawardene off the bowling of off-spinner Colin Miller, Waugh running back from short fine leg, Gillespie charging in from deep backward square leg. Watching from the players' balcony, physiotherapist Errol Alcott anticipated the collision and was on the boundary edge with his emergency medical kit almost before it happened.

It was the Australian captain, Waugh, clutching the bridge of his bloodied and broken nose, who initially received most of the attention. Gillespie, although he remained sitting on the ground, appeared to be in less distress (Tony Greig, on commentary at the time, speculated over the airways that 'maybe his knee is buggered'). In fact, it was the pace man's left shin that had been shattered. Neither player, incidentally, had managed to catch the ball. A helicopter landed on the outfield to airlift the injured pair to a hospital in Colombo – an episode that in the words of *Wisden* was 'reminiscent of a scene out of *Apocalypse Now*.' Not one to stay out of the action for long, Steve Waugh, his nose still plastered, returned to lead his side in the second Test. His damaged fast bowler, however, was sidelined for several months.

Dental care

A snow-affected pitch at Buxton in a county match between Derbyshire and Lancashire in June, 1975 had the ball lifting dangerously off a length. Derbyshire batsman Ashley Harvey-Walker handed umpire Dickie Bird something wrapped in a handkerchief. It was his false teeth. The generally jovial Harvey-Walker, sometimes called Ashley Hearty-Whacker because of his strong-arm tactics with the bat, didn't stay long at the crease, being dismissed for just seven. On his way back to the pavilion he collected his teeth from the umpire.

Last hurrah

The combined age of Brian Close and John Edrich as they walked out to open England's second innings against West Indies at Old Trafford in 1976 was 84. There was just 65 minutes' play left on Saturday (the third day) and the home side had been set the small task of scoring 552 to win. Given that they had been blown apart for 71 in the first innings by the West Indian trio of fast bowlers – Michael Holding (5 for 17), Andy Roberts (3 for 22) and Wayne Daniel (2 for 13) – few gave them much of a chance. All three speed merchants routinely topped 145 kph (90 mph) and the two batsmen knew they were in for a torrid time.

Neither was unused to the painful effects of fast bowling. Edrich had had two ribs broken by Dennis Lillee a couple of years before, and Close had unflinchingly stood up to Wes Hall and Charlie Griffith at their fastest at Lord's in 1963, a match in which Colin Cowdrey had suffered a broken arm. Like two old gunfighters facing a final showdown, the veteran pair (without helmets, arm guards or chest protectors) were subjected to a barrage of viciously targeted, short-pitched bowling. When Edrich asked his partner between overs what he thought was the best way to play it, Close replied, 'With your chest'. And so they did. When they returned to the dressing room at the close of play, their wickets still intact, both sported an array of shocking bruises to prove it. They put on 54 for the first wicket, then watched as England disintegrated once more, all out for 126 (Roberts 6 for 37). Neither player was called upon by his country again.

Close call

Australian batsman Graham Yallop was the first player to wear a helmet in a Test match. It was 1978. Sixteen years before, the Indian opener Nari Contractor almost died when struck on the head by a ball from Charlie Griffith in a tour match against Barbados. It took two major operations to save Contractor's life – West Indies captain Frank Worrell being the first to donate blood for a transfusion. Although he eventually returned to first-class cricket (with a steel plate in his skull), Contractor's Test career was knocked on the head.

Freak injuries

Middlesex and England off-spinner Fred Titmus had four toes
sliced off his left foot by a boat's propeller while swimming
in the sea during the 1967–68 tour of the West Indies.
Amazingly, he was playing cricket eight weeks later.

New Zealand all-rounder Trevor Franklin suffered
multiple leg fractures when he was mowed down by a
motorised baggage trolley at Gatwick Airport in 1986,
keeping him out of the game for 18 months.

The England all-rounder Chris Lewis was dubbed 'The Prat
without a Hat' by *The Sun* newspaper after he suffered severe
sunstroke during a match against Antigua in 1994, having taken
the field without any protective covering on his shaven head.

In 2006, Australian opener Matthew Hayden was attacked by a
dog while jogging near his home and sustained a 5-cm gash on
his ankle. At the time he'd been recovering from a broken finger.

When Ted Dexter's car ran out of petrol in West London
in 1965, the former England captain decided to push
it. He lost control of the vehicle which rolled back on to
him and crushed his leg, cutting short his Test career.

Stumped for stumpers

Four players kept wicket for England in the Lord's Test against New Zealand in 1986, but only two of them were in the chosen 11. During England's first innings, on the second morning, wicketkeeper Bruce French was struck on the head by a bouncer from Richard Hadlee. He was forced to retire and when shortly afterwards England took the field, teammate Bill Athey donned the gloves for the opening overs. In the meantime, England recruited their former stumper, the 45-year-old Bob Taylor, who was at the ground working for the match sponsor Cornhill in their hospitality suite. Taylor kept wicket impeccably for 76 overs before he in turn was replaced by Hampshire 'keeper Bobby Parks, summoned to Lord's on one of his rare days off. The substitutions were courtesy of the remarkably accommodating New Zealand skipper Jeremy Coney.

Ten tips for preventing injuries

 Always warm up before a game or practice session.

 Wear protective gear in the nets as well as when out in the middle.

 Make sure your protective equipment fits securely and is adequate for the task.

 Wear cricket boots that are comfortable and give proper support, with studs that grip on a damp surface.

 Maintain a good level of fitness during the off-season.

 Don't be tempted to play if you are carrying a minor injury since it will simply aggravate it.

 Make sure that there is always a first-aid kit on hand, along with someone experienced in using it.

 Young bowlers especially should receive proper coaching advice about their bowling action, to avoid long-term back stress.

 Don't imitate professional cricketers too closely, especially when it comes to diving about in the field: they get paid to take risks.

 Always wear sunscreen, and a cap or sunhat if you are a bit thin on top!

CHAPTER 11

SOME
TIGHT FINISHES

Cricket is a game played on the edges of the nerves.
PETER ROEBUCK (EX-SOMERSET PLAYER AND CRICKET WRITER)

No one who saw the final dramatic stages, at the ground or on television, of the Edgbaston Test against Australia in 2005 is likely to forget it in a hurry. Among the heroes for England, winners by just two runs, were Marcus Trescothick and Kevin Pietersen with the bat, and the inspirational Andrew Flintoff with both bat and ball. For Australia, Shane Warne turned in another memorable performance, and towards the end Brett Lee and Michael Kasprowicz came close to turning a probable loss into an improbable victory.

It was cricket at its gripping best and had spectators perched on the edge of their seats – as did these other games that went down to the wire.

Vital run

The first Test between South Africa and England at Durban in 1948; South Africa batted first, totalling a modest 161. England's two opening bowlers, Alec Bedser of Surrey and Cliff Gladwin of Derbyshire, shared seven wickets between them. Len Hutton (83) and Denis Compton (72) were the top scorers in England's reply of 253 – a useful first-innings lead of 92.

When the home side was dismissed for just 219 in their second innings, the match seemed to be in the bag: only 128 required for victory. But England lost wickets steadily. They were 52 for 3, then 70 for 6, with only the tail left. The man who had done the damage was South Africa's debutant fast bowler Cuan McCarthy. The 19-year-old from Natal finished with figures of 6 for 43, which would prove to be his best Test return.

When Gladwin joined Bedser at the wicket the score was 116 for 8. Twelve runs more needed to win. By the start of the final (eight-ball) over, to be bowled by Lindsay Tuckett, the target had been whittled down to eight runs. Bedser brought the scores level off the sixth ball, with any one of four results still possible. Gladwin had a heave at the seventh ball but missed it entirely.

The two batsmen conferred mid-pitch and decided to run on the next ball, come what may. As Tuckett ran in to bowl the fielders closed in ready to prevent a single. Gladwin had another fruitless swipe at the ball, which rapped him on the pad and bounced a yard or two in front of him. The bespectacled South African spinner 'Tufty' Mann lunged at it from short-leg, but not quickly enough. Bedser and Gladwin, neither of whom was known for his agility, scampered through for the vital run. England were the victors by two wickets.

Gloomy ending

In July 1971, Lancashire met Gloucestershire in the semi-final of the Gillette Cup at Old Trafford in front of a crowd of 24,000, with millions more watching on television. The visitors batted first and made 229 for 6 in their 60 overs, the South African all-rounder Mike Procter top scoring with 65.

Set to make just under four runs an over to win, Lancashire began steadily, their England opening pair of David Lloyd and Barry Wood putting on 61 for the first wicket. West Indies captain Clive Lloyd contributed a useful 34, but wickets continued to fall, and with five overs in the match remaining, the home side, with just three wickets left, needed 25 runs for victory.

It was nearly 9 p.m. (an hour after lunch was lost through rain) and there were no floodlights, though the lights were on in the pavilion and in the surrounding streets. In the advancing gloom Gloucestershire captain Tony Brown threw the ball to former England off-spinner John Mortimore, who already had three wickets to his name.

Batsman David Hughes briefly conferred with his own skipper Jack Bond, the non-striker, before shaping to face the first ball of the 56th over. He hit it for six and then followed with four, two, two, four and six – 24 runs off the over. By now it was so dark that many in the crowd (and on the field) were unable to see where the ball was hit but were guided by the cheers of those who could. The winning run, struck by Bond, came off the fifth ball of the next over and Lancashire were home by three wickets. Six weeks later they lifted the Gillette Cup at Lord's.

Dressing down

At close of play on the second day of the county match between Hampshire and Nottinghamshire at Southampton in May 1930, the home side required just one run to win. The extra half hour had been taken but the Notts captain A. W. Carr refused to continue beyond that, even though victory for his opponents was a formality. The next morning the Nottinghamshire side took the field in their travelling clothes, a couple of the players wearing overcoats to ward off the chill. The winning run was mercifully struck off the second ball of the day.

In a spin

Rain had reduced the County Championship match between Sussex and Surrey at Eastbourne in August 1972 to little more than two days. But in front of a holiday crowd both teams did their best to keep the game alive. Surrey, batting first, scored 300 for 4 before declaring. Then sporting declarations by both captains set up a run chase for the home side of 205 in 135 minutes to win. A big second-wicket partnership between Geoffrey Greenidge and Roger Prideaux (who had made a century in the first innings) took Sussex to 187 for 1, with three overs remaining. Eighteen to get, at a run a ball seemed a formality.

With the first ball of the next over, the Surrey and England off-spinner Pat Pocock bowled Greenidge: 187 for 2. His third ball bowled Mike Buss and after conceding two runs from the fourth, he caught and bowled Jim Parks off the last. It was 189 for 4. Eleven runs came off the following over bowled by Robin Jackman. Sussex needed five runs from the final over with Prideaux (97 not out) on strike.

Pocock dismissed Prideaux with the first ball and Griffith with the second, completing a hat-trick. Five runs were required from four balls with four wickets standing. The new batsman Jeremy Morley was stumped off the next ball and Pocock had taken four in four and six in nine (a world record). A run came from the fourth ball; then Tony Buss was bowled by the fifth. Off the last ball of the game Uday Joshi was run out going for a second run. Match drawn, with Sussex 202 for 9 at the close. It was the first time that five wickets had fallen in a final over, with Pocock's 7 wickets (for 4 runs) in 11 balls yet another world record.

Second time around

The 1986 Madras Test was the first in the three-match series between India and Australia. Allan Border won the toss for the visitors, who batted through the first two days, finally declaring on 574 for 7 (Dean Jones 210, David Boon 122, Border 106). A century from captain Kapil Dev (119) enabled the home side to reach 397 all out, giving Australia a substantial lead of 177. Border then declared Australia's second innings at their overnight total of 170 for 5, setting India a target of 348 to win on the final day.

At tea, India were 193 for 2, with Sunil Gavaskar still at the crease. With another 30 overs still to go and 8 wickets in hand, the home side was well placed to pull off a surprising victory. Gavaskar fell for 90, but Mohinder Amarnath, Mohammad Azharuddin and Chandra Pandit all made useful contributions and when the sixth wicket fell at 331, only 17 more runs were needed. Australia's two spinners, Ray Bright and Greg Matthews, who had taken all the wickets thus far, then dismissed Chetan Sharma, wicketkeeper Kiran More and Shivlal Yadav. When last man Maninder Singh came to the wicket eight balls were left and four runs required.

The combative off-spinner Matthews prepared to bowl the last over. On strike was Ravi Shastri, 45 not out. He hit a two, then a single to level the scores, leaving Maninder Singh three balls in which to make the winning run. The turbaned left-arm spinner defended the first and was out, leg before, to the second. For only the second time in cricket history a Test match was tied. And once again, Australia was involved.

Cup nerves

Edgbaston was the venue for the second semi-final of the 1999 World Cup: Australia v South Africa. Australia lost the toss and were put into bat. At 68 for 4 South Africa were decidedly on top but a partnership of 90 between captain Steve Waugh (56) and Michael Bevan (65) helped the Aussies to a respectable 213 from their 50 overs. South Africa's pace bowlers did most of the damage, Shaun Pollock taking 5 for 36, Allan Donald 4 for 32.

The South African innings followed a remarkably similar pattern to that of their opponents. The Proteas were 61 for 4 (three of them to Shane Warne) before Jacques Kallis (53) and Jonty Rhodes (43) put on 84 together. Pollock added a further valuable 20 runs, and when he was the seventh batsman out the score stood at 183. Thirty-one required to win (a tie would see Australia through to the final as they had the better record in the Super Sixes). Importantly for South Africa the destructive Lance Klusener was still there.

Two more wickets fell: Mark Boucher bowled by Glenn McGrath and Steve Elworthy run out. Allan Donald was last man in. Nine runs were required as Damien Fleming began the final over. Klusener smashed the first two balls to the boundary, levelling the scores with still four deliveries to go. He mishit the fourth ball to Mark Waugh at mid off and galloped down the pitch for what would be the winning run. Donald, who had narrowly missed being run out the ball before, was slow to move. Waugh threw the ball to Fleming who rolled it to wicketkeeper Adam Gilchrist at the other end. The tardy Donald, dropping his bat in the excitement, was stranded midway. Australia were through to the final.

CHAPTER 12

IT'S NOT CRICKET

Cricket is a gentleman's game, not a contact sport.
NIRANJAN SHAH (BOARD OF CONTROL FOR CRICKET IN INDIA)

The Hansie Cronje match-fixing scandal of 2000 and the notorious no-ball incident at Lord's ten years later, which resulted in jail sentences for three Pakistani players – Salman Butt, Mohammad Asif and Mohammad Amir – brought the game into disrepute and tarnished the reputations of several other international cricketers. In the burgeoning years of the sport, gambling was part of the scene but its recurrence in modern times has had uglier connotations. That said, the game flourishes at many levels around the world and conduct unbecoming – aside from some ritual sledging on the field – remains comparatively rare.

Occasionally, though, it's simply not cricket.

Watering the pitch

Controversy broke out during the third Test between Australia and England at Melbourne in 1955. For some time the pitch at the MCG had been causing problems for batsmen, with half-inch cracks opening up after just a couple of days' play. A new curator (groundsman) had been appointed to sort things out, but whatever steps he had taken appeared not to have worked. By day two of the Test the cracks had resurfaced.

The series was crucially poised at one all, Australia having won the first Test at Brisbane and England the next at Sydney. With the current match at the halfway stage, things were finely balanced. England had been dismissed in their first innings for 191 and Australia were 188 for 8 at close of play on Saturday. Sunday was a rest day. There had been much talk about the parlous state of the pitch, but when play got underway again on Monday the cracks had mysteriously closed up – just in time for England's second innings. Batting on a more benign surface England made 279 (Peter May falling nine runs short of a century in consecutive Tests), setting Australia a target of 240 to win. But by the time it was Australia's turn to bat again, the pitch had dried and the cracks had reappeared. Aided and abetted by the wickedly uneven bounce the frighteningly fast Frank 'Typhoon' Tyson (7 for 27) was virtually unplayable, and Australia were despatched for 111. England went one up in the series, which they eventually took 3–1 to retain the Ashes. After the match there was the inevitable post-mortem with accusations flying in all directions. But neither the curator nor anyone else owned up to having done a spot of watering.

Tactical error

Worcestershire and Somerset met in a Group A fixture during the 1979 Benson & Hedges 55-overs competition. The match had been scheduled for the day before but rain at New Road had delayed the start. Somerset, as leaders of their group, were on course for a place in the quarter-final, but in the final analysis it could all come down to which team had the best strike rate. In order to preserve Somerset's current standing in that regard, their captain and opening batsman Brian Rose declared his side's innings closed after one over, with the score at one (a no-ball). Worcestershire, in the form of their New Zealand overseas player Glenn Turner, then scored the necessary two runs to win and the match was over in a matter of minutes.

Angry spectators, including many Somerset supporters who had made the long journey up the M5 in anticipation of a keenly fought contest, expressed their displeasure. Rose was widely condemned in the media, though he remained unrepentant, claiming that he had acted strictly within the rules. However, his success at manipulating the result was short-lived. At a specially convened meeting of the Test and County Cricket Board a few days later, Somerset was expelled from the competition for not conforming to the spirit of the game. Two years later they lifted the B&H trophy at Lord's, unquestionable champions.

Foreign input

No fewer than seven of the England team that took the field for the first Test against New Zealand at Christchurch in 1992 had been born outside the UK: Graeme Hick (Rhodesia), Robin Smith and Allan Lamb (South Africa), Dermot Reeve (Hong Kong), Chris Lewis (Guyana), Derek Pringle (Kenya) and Phillip DeFreitas (Dominica).

What a riot!

Rioting broke out after tea on the third day of the second Test between West Indies and England at Port-of-Spain, Trinidad, in 1960. In reply to England's first-innings total of 382, West Indies were struggling at 98 for 7, thanks to some magnificent fast bowling from Fred Trueman and Brian Statham who shared six wickets between them. In contrast to the constant, often wayward, short-pitched bowling of their opponents, the England pair had kept the ball up to the batsmen, generating swing and movement off the pitch. A restlessly disappointed crowd of 30,000 – a record for any sporting event in the Caribbean – watched the cream of West Indian batting brushed aside.

Enter a local favourite, left-arm spinner Charran Singh, who was making his Test debut. Almost at once he was run out by a sharp throw from Ted Dexter at cover. It was a signal for bottles, cans and other missiles to be hurled onto the field. England's captain Peter May summoned his players into the middle for safety, where six of them armed themselves with stumps. Together with the not out batsman Sonny Ramadhin, another local hero, May approached the angry spectators and appealed for calm, but to no avail. Reluctantly, he led his team off the field, escorted by uniformed sailors from the royal yacht *Britannia*, which had been making a courtesy visit to the island. Play resumed the following day but, with no change of fortune for the home side, England won the match by 256 runs.

Close encounter

Two of the most abrasive players of the modern era, Dennis Lillee and Javed Miandad, were involved in an ugly confrontation at Perth in 1981, on the fourth day of the first Test against Pakistan. Things had not been going Pakistan's way,

having been dismissed for 62 (Lillee 5 for 18) in reply to Australia's first innings total of 180. The home side had made a better fist of their second innings, clocking up 424 and setting their opponents a well-nigh impossible 543 to win. They were an unpromising 27 for 2 when skipper Miandad came in to bat.

Neither Lillee nor Miandad were strangers to controversy. Both were brilliant but extremely volatile cricketers. Some would say a flashpoint between them was inevitable. It came when Miandad, running a comfortable single, collided with Lillee, the bowler. Accounts differ as to who started what, and why. Lillee appeared to impede the Pakistan captain and then kick him; Miandad in response wielded his bat like a club in Lillee's direction. Before the two men could come to blows, umpire Tony Crafter stepped in and separated them as if in a boxing ring. Most observers, including several former Australian captains, blamed Lillee for the incident (Bobby Simpson describing it as 'the most disgraceful thing I have seen on a cricket field'), though Miandad was hardly faultless. The ill-feeling lingered throughout the series. Lillee received a derisory AU$120 fine and a two-match ban (two minor ODIs). Miandad got off scot-free. Australia won the three-match series, but cricket itself was the loser.

Six of the best

The man at the centre of the storm was match referee Mike Denness, a former England captain. He was officiating at the second Test between South Africa and India at Port Elizabeth in 2001, and during the course of the game cited six Indian players for misconduct. Three of them – spinner Harbhajan Singh, batsman Shiv Sunder Das and wicketkeeper Deep Dasgupta – received suspended one-match bans for excessive appealing. Virender Sehwag was banned for one Test for aggressively claiming a catch off Jacques Kallis when the ball had patently bounced in front of him, and the captain Sourav Ganguly a similar penalty for not controlling his team.

But the most controversial citing was that of Sachin Tendulkar for ball tampering. The television cameras had captured Tendulkar picking at the seam of the ball when bowling, though he claimed to be merely cleaning it (an action to which he should have drawn the umpire's attention). Uproar broke out, with India's cricket board at loggerheads with the ICC, who backed their match referee. There were accusations of racism, and when the Indian and South African boards usurped the ICC's role and replaced Denness for the next Test, the ICC designated the match 'unofficial'. In India, effigies of Denness were burnt in the streets and there were threats of cancelling the forthcoming tour of England. In the event, the bans issued to Tendulkar and Ganguly were lifted, with only Sehwag having to sit out his punishment.

Immoral delivery

The googly (see p.155) made a dramatic, though not entirely faultless, entry into cricket history. The inventor of this off-break bowled with a leg-break action was Middlesex all-rounder Bernard Bosanquet, who unleashed his mystery ball in a county match against Leicestershire in 1900. The ball bounced four times before reaching the batsman Sammy Coe who was stumped, in more ways than one, for 98. Two years later Bosanquet was a member of the MCC side that toured Australia under Pelham Warner. In the match against New South Wales he clean bowled the great Victor Trumper with the first-ever googly seen in Australia. Thereafter the googly was known down under as a 'Bosie'. Bosanquet later said of his devious delivery, 'It was not unfair; only immoral'.

Protest stopped play

In 1975, campaigners demanding the release of convicted armed robber George Davis, a former east London mini-cab driver, vandalised the Headingley pitch during the third Test against Australia. The event had been targeted because of its high profile, not because Davis or his supporters had any association with cricket. Three-inch holes were dug in the middle and oil poured over the wicket at the rugby club end before the start of the final day. The walls outside the ground were daubed with pro-Davis slogans from what had been an ongoing national campaign.

The match, tantalisingly poised, was abandoned as a draw with Australia on 220 for 3 in their second innings, chasing what would have been a record-winning total of 445 for victory. Opener Rick McCosker was left stranded five short of a maiden Test century. Earlier in the game Middlesex left-arm spinner Phil Edmonds had made an auspicious Test debut, taking 5 for 28 in Australia's first innings; and England's hero of the summer, the prematurely grey, bespectacled and helmetless David Steele, had defied the Aussie pace quartet of Dennis Lillee, Jeff Thomson, Gary Gilmour and Max Walker, top-scoring in both innings with 73 and 92. Australia went on to retain the Ashes, winning the four-match series 1-0. Four people were arrested for the assault on the Headingley pitch. As for George Davis himself, he was released from jail in 1976 but back behind bars two years later following another robbery, for which he pleaded guilty – to the undoubted relief of cricket administrators and supporters.

10 other things that have stopped play

A swarm of bees had players lying face down during the first Test between Sri Lanka and England at Kandy in 2007.

During an Australia v Pakistan ODI at Trent Bridge in 2001, a Pakistan supporter threw a firework onto the field, prompting the Australian team to walk off.

In 2013, badgers dug up the pitch at the Rickmansworth Cricket Club in Hertfordshire.

A bomb scare halted play at Lord's in 1973 during the Test match against West Indies.

The gloved Derbyshire wicketkeeper had to remove a prickly hedgehog from the pitch during a county match against Gloucestershire in 1957.

During the Sydney Test against England in 1982–83, a fan released a pig onto the outfield. It was branded 'Botham' on one side and 'Eddie' [Hemmings] on the other.

 Start of play on the third day of the India v England Test at Delhi in 1981–82 was delayed when the key to the ball cupboard was mislaid.

 A venomous red-bellied black snake brought things to a standstill during an under-17 game near Sydney in 2009.

 Players hit the ground during a wartime match at Lord's between the Army and the RAF in 1944 when a flying bomb seemed to be heading their way.

 Dazzling evening sun forced players from the field at Derby during a day-nighter against Notts in 2006.

CONCLUSION – A VIEW FROM THE BOUNDARY

The public want to see people play an exciting brand of cricket.
SHANE WARNE (AUSTRALIA)

Over the 300 years of its recorded history, cricket has shown itself to be a resilient and adaptable sport, and one that continues to attract new adherents. In addition to the ten Test-playing nations, there are currently 37 ICC associate members – Israel, Germany and Japan improbably among them – and, spanning the globe, a further 60 affiliate members. Who knows, if the spirit of cricket is allowed to prevail there might be hope for the world after all.

But despite the game's missionary spread, its future direction at the professional level is far from clear. Since the inaugural match in Melbourne in 1877, Test cricket has been universally recognised as the pre-eminent expression of the sport and for players the ultimate accolade. However, Ashes series aside and with England in general the honourable exception, crowds at Test matches are declining. Television coverage in South Africa, India, New Zealand, Sri Lanka and the Caribbean regularly displays a backdrop of woefully empty stands.

In brazenly sharp contrast, the Indian Premier League and Australia's Big Bash play their Twenty20 fixtures in front of packed houses.

The financial balance of power, along with the spectators, is shifting from Test cricket to the shorter format – the new kid on the block – and with it political muscle within the ICC. There are fears of a serious rift developing as the richer countries push for a greater say in the running of the game. Words like 'brand', 'product' and 'merchandise' have become part of cricket's vocabulary.

Most commentators would agree that there is too much Test cricket being played (indeed too much cricket of any sort). Because of the gulf between the strongest and weakest sides there has been talk of dividing the ten Test countries into two leagues, with promotion and relegation, broadly along the lines of English county cricket. But since the ICC consists of representatives of the national cricket boards, opposition to a two-tier structure that would inevitably diminish those banished to the lower league is bound to be fierce.

The long-awaited World Test Championship involves only the four top-ranked countries; in recent years, South Africa, England, Australia and India – despite the latter's puzzlingly poor record away from home. Among the others, Bangladesh and Zimbabwe struggle to make significant progress at Test level; the glory days of West Indies have become a distant memory; and with little sign of security returning to their homeland any time soon, the nomadic Pakistan team has been forced to pitch its tent in the United Arab Emirates, though they still remain a formidable side.

Whatever adjustments are made to the Test scene (the concern being that if nothing is done Test cricket will follow the dinosaur into extinction), the Ashes rivalry seems set to continue. That said, you can still have too much of a good thing and a greedily overcrowded programme of Test matches, ODIs and Twenty20 fixtures, even between the two oldest belligerents, tests the stamina of players and fans alike. All too often, it seems, the greatest threat to the game's survival comes from the sport's administrators.

The impact of Twenty20 cricket has been as great on the field as off. Improvisation is the name of the game, with players adapting their tactics and techniques to achieve success, often with spectacular results. This brash addition to cricket's repertoire has inevitably caught the imagination of younger fans, their enthusiasm undented by the monotonous choreography of the dancing girls at the boundary edge. If the cash-rich leagues continue to prosper, the next generation of young cricketers could well make Twenty20 their principal focus, reducing the pool of talent for Test matches. One way or another, nocturnal cricket with its glitzy mix (unpalatable to some) of sport and showbiz seems destined to run and run.

Lacking the gravitas of Test cricket or the flair of Twenty20, the 50-overs game is looking somewhat old hat, not least during the stuttering early stages of the four-yearly World Cup. Routinely tacked on either end of a Test series, the fixtures are like guests who turn up to a party too soon or linger long after it is all over. If the international load needs to be lightened – and it does – the administrators could begin by culling the ubiquitous ODI.

On the domestic front, county cricket has been restructured once again, but fundamental problems remain. With the country's top players contracted to the ECB, and others lining their pockets in the Indian Premier League, the counties have been forced to call on the services of overseas mercenaries, who make their exits and entrances with bewildering speed. The four-day game, the breeding ground for England's Test cricketers, is increasingly under threat, largely unwatched and heavily subsidised. One possible solution could be to leave the more profitable limited-overs competitions in the hands of the counties and for first-class cricket to be played only on a regional basis, with fewer fixtures and higher standards. But with county chairmen and their committees possessively defending their fiefdoms, this is easier said than done.

The game's administrators and pundits will doubtless continue to ponder these and other problems, to good or bad effect. Happily, whatever the decisions of the powers that be, cricket at the grass roots will remain largely undisturbed. On village greens and in urban parks, on close-cut playing fields and in sheep-shorn meadows, and wherever else cricketers of all ages can cheerfully engage with bat and ball, there will be nothing more at stake than the inherent joy of the summer game itself.

LANGUAGE OF CRICKET

The origins of some of cricket's idiosyncratic terms are difficult to pin down with absolute certainty, but these are the most likely explanations:

Bail
A sixteenth-century term for a crossbar used to hold something in place; e.g. the top of a gate. (See Wicket).

Bat
From the Old English word batt, meaning 'club, stick or staff'.

Chinaman
The left-arm bowler's off-break to a right-hander. An unorthodox delivery that was politically incorrectly associated with the stereotype of a cunning Chinaman.

Crease
Before the introduction of painted white lines in the second half of the nineteenth century the crease was a furrow cut in the turf.

Googly
From the notion that the ball so mystified batsmen that it made their eyes 'goggle' or (in some dialects) 'google'.

Gully
The channel or 'gully' between the slips and point.

Hat-trick
On having achieved the feat, the bowler would be rewarded with a new hat or a hat would be passed among spectators for a collection.

Maiden over
'Maiden' in the sense of unproductive (e.g. a maiden aunt).

Point
Originally called 'point of the bat', the fielder in this position was almost within reach of the end of the striker's bat.

Popping crease

To complete a 'notch' or run, batsmen originally had to place their bat in a shallow hole in front of the stumps. If the wicketkeeper or fieldsman popped the ball into the hole before the batsman could reach it, the latter was deemed run out. Hand injuries to fielders colliding with the bat in the popping hole eventually led to the modern demarcation line.

Wicket

A wicket gate is often part of, or next to, a larger gate built into a fence or wall. Shepherds playing a primitive form of the game on the downs probably used the gate of a sheep pen as a 'wicket'.

Yorker

'York' and 'Yorkshire' have historical slang connotations of sharp practice. To be 'yorked' was to be deceived – the fate of any batsman dismissed by a yorker.

THE JOY OF GOLF

RAY HAMILTON

THE JOY OF GOLF

Ray Hamilton

ISBN: 978 1 84953 598 4   Hardback   £9.99

I don't play too much golf.
Two rounds a day are plenty.
HARRY VARDON

This pocket-sized miscellany, packed with fascinating facts, handy hints and captivating stories and quotes from the world of golf, is perfect for anyone who knows the incomparable joy of hitting the fairway.

If you're interested in finding out more about our books,
find us on Facebook at **Summersdale Publishers** and
follow us on Twitter at **@Summersdale.**

www.summersdale.com